MAKING
DISCIPLES

How did Jesus do it?

TONY PULLIN
CWR

Practical, inspirational and birthed by years of the greatest schooling possible – actually doing discipleship – Tony opens the way to the only ultimate purpose of Christianity: disciple making that will produce kingdom-focused world changers. Highly recommended.
Jeff Lucas, author, speaker and broadcaster

Tony Pullin's inspiring and liberating approach to this vital subject for today, with his spoken and unspoken emphasis on God's grace, makes compelling reading both for groups seeking to grow together or individuals. I cannot recommend it more highly.
Sandy Millar, founder of Alpha

It is my belief that this book addresses two of the most pressing needs in church life today, discipleship and culture. *Making Disciples* practically connects the Jesus model of discipleship with today's world. The culture in which discipleship takes place can turn theory into a productive lifestyle for growing churches.
Stuart Bell, Senior Pastor of New Life Lincoln; leader of the Ground Level Network

One of the vital needs of twenty-first century churches is to deepen and develop the way we lead people who come to know Christ into daily discipleship. Tony Pullin's emphasis and focus on Jesus' discipling of His followers, and on the way they then put that into practice as the church began to grow and expand, provide helpful pointers for today's church leaders together with thought-provoking questions for group discussion.
Mark Bailey, Lead Pastor of Trinity Cheltenham; New Wine Leadership Team

Doing it the way Jesus did. If we put into practice the principles in this book we will nurture and inspire a new generation of followers of Jesus to be disciple-making disciples.
Philip Deller, Senior Minister of Chipping Campden Baptist Church; FreshStreams Network Leadership Team

Can there be a greater or more important challenge for the twenty-first century church? Tony Pullin's book faces up to the great directive that Jesus gave to his followers to 'go make disciples'. With lots of practical advice and provocative questions, I'm sure it will become an important part of the Church's response to his commission in our generation.
Steve Clifford, General Director of Evangelical Alliance

An invaluable book looking at the vital issue of discipleship. Get it, read it and live it!
Gavin Calver, National Director of British Youth for Christ

Discipleship is a key area of growth in the church today, and yet it is so often over-intellectualised. Tony writes simply, personally and powerfully about Jesus' invitation to us to become his disciples. Discipleship, Tony suggests, is about moving forward a step at a time, discovering the heart of Jesus, learning to enjoy the presence of God, being helped to live from the Spirit within, and being taught from Scripture what pleases the Lord – and all this not alone but in companionship with others. I often think that if we get the simple things right, the complicated things will look after themselves – and this book is a demonstration of that.

Rev Dr Alison Morgan, ReSource Team

I have long felt that Tony Pullin should translate his years of experience and teaching into written form, accessible to a wider audience. I believe that this work, his first offering, is the right book at the right time – a must for every church which is serious about fulfilling their God-given destiny and their part in the Great Commission of Jesus.

John Noble, Pioneer and Chair of the National Charismatic Leaders Conference 1984–2006

Discipleship is on everyone's agenda. Denominations and churches realise that in today's culture, who we are speaks a great deal louder than what we say. This fantastic book gives a practical overview of discipleship from a biblical perspective but is also filled with many stories that illustrate how discipleship works in today's church and culture.

Laurence Singlehurst, Director of Cell UK

This valuable book not only explores the greatest current need of the church of Christ but reveals, unsurprisingly, Jesus as the greatest mentor of all time, to be followed by those who are called to follow him. Thank you Tony, all denominations and streams could be revolutionised by this message and its practice.

Roger Forster, founder and leader of Ichthus Christian Fellowship

Somewhat confused, agnostic people feel they don't want to be preached at. Yet most are willing to be prayed for – some even in the high street and shopping centre of my home town! But we need much more than prayerful moments and initial decisions. We are in great need of whole lifestyle disciples! It is not sufficient to merely give people a Christian experience – rather we are to help make sense of what it means to love and therefore obey Christ, which sometimes fails to provide us with short term elated spiritual feelings!

This rare book, simply written, well researched and full of good quotes, is way overdue. So little has been written of discipleship of late, but this publication will help ensure a strong, relevant future for God's people, the Church. So read, absorb, influence and lead – whether that be one person or many. Profile does not equal importance – you have no idea who you have under your care, or who they will become in the future. So believe the best and be intentional with love, sensitivity, truthfulness and instruction, always pointing to the Great Discipler – Jesus Christ!

Gerald Coates, speaker, author and broadcaster

Tony Pullin is a very gifted writer, but far and above that simple statement is the reader's rapid recognition that there is a wealth of excellent teaching, experience and insight behind the words on every page of this remarkable book. The subject, 'Making Disciples', is a vital one for us all and the approach taken in two distinct parts, 'Masterclass' and 'A Discipling Community', is enriching, stimulating and enormously helpful in developing a fuller Scriptural understanding of discipleship. Part Two is both realistic and practical after the Masterclass of Part One.

I found that the reflections at the end of every chapter challenged my own thinking and anchored the teaching in my mind in very practical and memorable ways. I finished reading the book utterly convinced that in the whole area of discipleship I really am equipped to be and do what that Lord has called me to be and do – in the author's own words, 'The Master still calls and his grace is still outrageous'.

This book should be compulsory reading for every Christian who wants to become a better disciple and to help others in their journey of discipleship. After reading it I found myself in full agreement with Dietrich Bonhoeffer who said that 'discipleship means joy'. Reading *Making Disciples* was a joy and I am quite certain that putting the teaching into practice will be an even greater joy.

Charles Whitehead, Chair of the International Charismatic Consultation on World Evangelisation; Chair of Catholic Evangelisation Services

There is one word on the lips of Canadian pastors, one unrelenting question. How can we disciple those in our churches to live fully passionate lives for Christ? This is a profound book that endorses the true nature of what twenty-first century discipleship must be; Tony Pullin shows us the Jesus way, with true authenticity.

Phil Collins, Senior Pastor of Willow Park Church, Kelowna, BC, Canada

I've known, loved, appreciated and worked with Tony Pullin for years. The book reflects the man. It is gracious, real, pertinent and wise. It is also practical and direct. If you know your dream demands discipleship and development, then read this book, and live it.

Pete Gilbert, Team Leader of DNA

This book contains years of tried and tested wisdom gleaned from the pages of Scripture and illustrated with the stories of friends who are travelling the disciple's journey. The commission to make disciples never tires and needs communicating afresh to each new generation. Tony has written about discipleship in a way that will serve this generation well and I look forward to recommending it to the student world.

Rich Wilson, National Team Leader of Fusion

Acknowledgements

The inspiration and encouragement of John Noble led to the writing of this book and for this I am deeply grateful. My thanks are also due to Jeff Lucas, Dave and Rhian Day, Mark Warren-Smith and Dawn Charles, all of whom, like John, read the manuscript and made helpful suggestions which have improved the book. I would also like to thank Lynette Brooks of CWR, whose enthusiasm and commitment guided the project through to fulfilment.

To the men and women of God who, over the years, have influenced my life, I say thank you for the privilege of journeying with you.

To Muriel

Whose love and support

have been my strength

since the day we made our promises

Contents

A foreword about last words

It was a devastating moment.

We'd spent two wonderful Christmassy weeks with our son, daughter and amazing (we're biased) grandsons. We'd done it all: played hard, shopped till we dropped, boosted the local economy with our eating out habits, frolicked in the snow, and roasted marshmallows over a campfire. It was a wonderful time, and now we felt the heaviness that comes with the knowledge that all that is beautiful, at least this side of forever, is temporary.

Now, at the airport, it was time to say goodbye. We all had tickets. They were flying back to England, and Kay and I were bound for another destination (I won't say where, in case you haven't been to Hawaii). The London flight was on time, ours had been cancelled, so we told our family to go on ahead of us through security. We'd get ourselves onto another flight, and be through in a few minutes to say our fond goodbyes.

It wasn't that straightforward and took ages, so by the time we'd got to their gate, their plane was pushing back towards the runway, with them seated in it somewhere. We missed our goodbye. We had shared so many words and smiles over those two weeks, but somehow parting words of love had a greater significance, and we missed them. Kay cried for 45 minutes.

Jesus had a parting moment with his disciples. It was not a farewell, just a temporary goodbye; ultimately they would be reuniting with him in a great eternal homecoming. But parting words are chosen carefully. You try to summarise what really matters, to say something that has the greatest weight, you prioritise that which *must* be remembered. I love you. Thank you. Be safe. Don't forget to do that. The key's under the mat.

Jesus' parting shot went like this: 'go and make disciples of all nations'. That was his final verbal legacy before taking to the clouds.

The words are very familiar. But what do they mean? How should we go about the business of making disciples?

In the book you're holding, Tony Pullin offers some practical, inspirational answers to those vital questions. Birthed by years of the greatest schooling possible – actually doing discipleship – Tony opens the way to the only ultimate purpose of Christianity: disciple making that will produce kingdom-focused world changers.

His message is urgent, but his tone breathes grace. He never trashes what is, in order to urge us towards what should be. Having worked alongside Tony in leadership development training for fifteen years, I know his heart, and it's tender. Tony's eyes fill with tears very frequently, especially when talking about his favourite subject – Jesus. And that's what put the icing on the cake for this book: the author is undeniably passionate, but caring. The warmth of the man comes through his words. I've read too many books that fill me with inspiration and hopelessness in turn, because they present an unattainable vision. But with Tony's gentle and quiet authority, we'll see a focused picture of a better – and reachable – future.

So go ahead. Read the book. Heed the advice. Take some further steps to fulfilling the instructions that Jesus gave in his final moments on this earth.

And Tony ...

Thanks.

Jeff Lucas

A word from John and Christine Noble

This book would be incomplete without a contribution from my friend and mentor of forty years, John Noble. Observing his life and ministry, I learned much about the Master's heart. John kindly acceded to my request and this is his response:

A valued friend and fellow traveller

Christine and I can look back to over fifty years in Christian ministry of one kind or another. During that time, it has always been a primary aim of ours to encourage those we meet along the way in our walk with Jesus. Some of those we have journeyed with have connected with us and us with them. As a result, lasting friendships have developed which, in turn, have led to a permanent commitment and working relationship. Sometimes this has involved a 'discipling' role.

In the context of these seemingly divine connections we have made it our mission to serve these brothers and sisters and help to release and, at times, resource them, so that they can discover and fulfil their God-given callings and ministries. Within these closer relationships, where love and respect have thrived, we have sought to add to encouragement the depth that mutual honesty and truthfulness can bring. At this point some cry off and the links dissolve; others struggle but hang in and ultimately learn from the experience; a few gladly embrace the challenge of facing up to issues and seeking the Lord for his wisdom.

Tony Pullin and his lovely wife, Muriel, have, without doubt, been the most open and responsive couple the Lord has placed us alongside. Not only have they welcomed our opinions and advice but have frequently sought us out to give input into both personal and ministry challenges, rather than waiting for us to approach them.

Tony is a great Bible teacher and over the years churches and individuals have benefited hugely from his insights and sensitive unfolding of scriptural truth. Many will remember with appreciation the years that Tony served Jeff Lucas in the 'Equipped to Lead' leadership training course in the Midlands. One thing I [John] had been talking to Tony about for some years was getting his teaching into book form. However, whilst he was open he had never felt clear about doing so, or about timing.

On 4 November 2012, at the annual Swanwick conference of Vision in Action (a Midlands network of churches within Pioneer), Tony brought a masterful and anointed message on discipleship. There was an immediate response and a standing ovation as the congregation recognised that this was a special God-moment – God had spoken! I had no hesitation in looking straight at Tony and prophesying that this was God's time for him to write. It was time for a book! Again there was tumultuous applause and the light went on in Tony's eyes. There were similar prophetic words from others, with the same clarity.

So, what we have here is Tony's response to a friend's encouragement and the Holy Spirit's confirmation – clear evidence of a true disciple of Jesus! Read and be blessed!

John and Christine Noble

Introduction

It came and went – the fireworks, the popping corks and the new millennium year. We found ourselves in the brave new world of the twenty-first century. We caught our breath and looked around us. Still longing, still committed, still praying, 'Lord, let your kingdom come!' Society continued to change, but faster. We tried to understand new challenges; serving Jesus in the midst of increasing social breakdown, economic meltdown and political disillusion. New forms of church continued to emerge; lots of things were being *re-imagined*, often helpfully. And despite the turbulent times, good news stories continued to happen across our nation, and still do.

And through it all, the Great Commission lives in our hearts. We still hear the words of Jesus, as clear today as when he spoke them in the first century: 'go and make disciples' (Matt. 28:19).

The age-long mandate doesn't change. Those words, which rang in the disciples' ears as they watched Jesus' feet leave the ground, pass their eye level and disappear above their heads into an unseen realm, still define our mission today. They are at the heart of Jesus' final instructions.

This book is an attempt to ask some questions about how we respond to what Jesus called us to do. What did he mean when he said, 'make disciples'? What did the Eleven understand by it? What does it mean to us in our time, with the constant challenge of finding our feet in a changing social landscape? If making disciples is more than spreading the good news and introducing others to Christ, how much more? What is our goal as we go about the task of fulfilling Jesus' command? How do we disciple others? In short: if making disciples was Jesus' primary strategy for growth, whether of the individual believer, the Church community, or, ultimately, the kingdom itself, are there fresh lessons to learn?

In our search for answers, the best starting point is to rewind a little and ask – how did Jesus do it? How did he take twelve ordinary people from different walks of life and shape them (bar one) to become foundational figures in the Church explosion which followed his return to heaven and the outpouring of the Spirit? Because whatever he did, that process was what the disciples must have understood by his parting words, 'go and make disciples'.

To discover more we are first going to travel with Jesus for a while, observing his relationship with the Twelve and the journey they shared. As we watch and listen, we will learn how we ourselves can be discipled and how, in turn, we can disciple others.

As Jesus-centred Church, we see in his life and teaching our example and guide. The closer our experience and practice is to Jesus, the closer we will be to the Father's heart and purposes. Jesus is the touchstone of all revelation. Paul urged the Christians at Colossae: 'Let the message of Christ dwell among you richly' (Col. 3:16). I think he was referring to the actual sayings and discourses of Jesus during his years of ministry.[1] These were remembered and passed on by those who heard him, circulated orally around the churches, until, as the first generation came to a close, they were recorded in the Gospels. Now we, too, can read the Gospel writers' accounts of 'all that Jesus began to do and to teach until the day he was taken up to heaven' (Acts 1:1–2). To understand the practice of discipleship, we can do no better than to observe and listen to the Master himself.

In Part One we will look at the example of a fellow disciple; walking our road, making our mistakes first, learning our lessons and loving the same Saviour and Friend. Identifying with Peter is not difficult! As we follow his remarkable journey, we will see the challenges, the changes, the growth, and ultimately, his emergence into the person Jesus called him to be. It will help us to understand the process by which Peter reached his destiny – an exciting process Jesus called discipleship.

So many practical lessons emerge about a discipling relationship. We learn how Jesus interacted with his sometimes errant, but always sincere, follower and how Peter responded to Jesus' input into his life. The character of the relationship and the stages of the journey unfold to present a compelling, real-life picture. And we see more clearly what Jesus meant when he said to the Eleven, 'go and make disciples' (Matt. 28:19).

In Part Two we will explore the questions which might naturally follow on from Part One. Is it possible to implement Jesus' model in the twenty-first century? Could it happen in *our* church? Would anything need to change first – if so, how would we go about that? What would a discipling community look like? What kind of leadership would we need?

I am forever grateful to have had the privilege of being discipled by someone I love and trust; whose encouragement and guidance helped me to develop as a person and as a ministry. Some of the lessons I learned, through failure and success alike, appear in the book, in the hope they will serve as windows into the nature of personal discipleship, in the setting of the believing community.

Some churches have introduced mentoring programmes as a means of encouraging personal growth – perhaps reflecting a felt need for one-to-one input and support. Mentoring ranges from formal structures to informal arrangements, each with its own definitions. It will mean different things to different people. For the sake of clarity, I have refrained from comparisons or contrasts between discipleship and mentoring. We will focus on exploring Jesus' example of training and teaching his disciples, and draw out its application to us today.

True discipleship has enormous potential. As always, taking Jesus' words seriously is dangerous and rewarding at the same time. But the Great Commission, still relevant to the twenty-first century, fireworks and all, remains a major key to the advance of God's kingdom.

So let's pack a travel bag and catch up with the group of twelve walking along the road with Jesus; chatting among themselves, laughing at each other's differences, asking him questions, listening to the Master. When they set out to follow him, they had no idea what lay ahead or how long the journey would last. As it turned out, it was just three years. Then it went cosmic.

---

1. See F.F. Bruce, *The Epistles to the Colossians, to Philemon, and to the Ephesians, The New International Commentary on the New Testament* (Eerdmans, 1984) p157, note 148.

PART ONE

MASTER-
CLASS

Chapter One
Meet me in Galilee

Revisiting the Great Commission

Discipleship doesn't come after mission – discipleship *is* our mission.

Imagine the emotions shared by the disciples that day, as they met with Jesus on one of the hills in Galilee. It was up here in 'Galilee of the Gentiles' that light had dawned and Jesus' ministry had begun (see Matt. 4:12–17): the first of many miracles, the teaching and preaching in the synagogues, the Sermon on the Mount and the healings. It was here that Jesus had called the Twelve to be with him and they had left everything to follow.

Then came the day that Jesus left Galilee for the last time and set off towards Jerusalem and suffering – and they had gone with him. Trying to understand, trying to make sense, holding on. They had lived through the trauma, the emotional blitz, of witnessing his arrest, his crucifixion and death; the mix of fear and elation as they discovered he was alive. And then the message to meet him back in Galilee. Galilee was special in their history: it had been home territory and the scene of so many memorable moments.

> Then the eleven disciples went to Galilee, to the mountain where Jesus had told them to go. When they saw him, they worshipped him; but some doubted.[1] Then Jesus came to them and said, 'All authority in heaven and on earth has been given to me. Therefore go and make disciples of all nations, baptising them in the name of the Father and of the Son and of the Holy Spirit, and teaching them to obey everything I have commanded you. And surely I am with you

always, to the very end of the age.'

(Matt. 28:16–20)

When we look again at the Great Commission we are faced with a remarkable challenge. First, Jesus declares the new reality: 'All authority in heaven and on earth has been given to me.' The kingdom of God had broken into first-century Palestine through the life and ministry of Jesus; the beachhead had been established in the Person of God's chosen King. And the cross had changed everything, with repercussions in the unseen world also. Now God had given Jesus universal sovereignty.

Standing in what God had given him, Jesus commissions the disciples. 'Therefore go and make disciples of all nations', literally, 'go and *disciple* the nations' – it's a verb: 'You go and *you* disciple others'. Essentially, Jesus said, 'What I have been doing for you over these last three years I want you to go and do in every nation'. He didn't need to spell it out – they knew exactly what he meant. They had experienced it. Jesus had invested in them, taking time to do it. They had shared meals together; he had encouraged them; he challenged their attitudes; he showed them how to live; he showed them how to serve; he gave them a chance to 'have a go'. He had *discipled* them.

Philip Vogel, a former Director of British Youth for Christ, writing in 1986 about developing leaders, suggests that 'the word most familiar to us, and that most aptly captures the essence of what it means to be a disciple, is "apprentice".'[2] Eugene Peterson adopted a similar approach in *The Message*: 'When Jesus saw his ministry drawing huge crowds, he climbed a hillside. Those who were apprenticed to him, the committed, climbed with him. Arriving at a quiet place, he sat down and taught his climbing companions' (Matt. 5:1–2). For Matthew 28:19 Peterson gives us, 'Go out and train everyone you meet, far and near, in this way of life'.

Before the time of Jesus, the word 'disciple' had been used to describe apprentices who were learning a trade. In Jesus' day it was associated with the disciples of a Rabbi, who would even live under his roof during the period of their training. The commission Jesus gave his disciples is about much more than leading others to Christ, wonderful as that is. It embraces an interpersonal process of discipleship – being helped to learn and grow, to become more like Jesus and to fulfil our calling to serve him. Donald Hagner put it this way: 'The word "disciple" means above all "learner" or "pupil". The emphasis in the commission thus falls not on the initial proclamation of the gospel but more on … nurturing into the experience of discipleship, an emphasis that is strengthened and explained by the instruction "teaching them to keep all that I have commanded".'[3]

Jesus didn't simply say, 'Go and tell them what I said', but, 'Go and teach them to obey what I said'. That is actually quite radical. Public teaching in the Church is enriching and helpful and part of the process, but discipleship is more than that. Paul wrote wonderful letters as well as teaching and preaching everywhere he went, but someone worked out that there were at least twenty-seven named people who travelled with him at one time or another. That tells us something about the value of personal discipleship. To be with Paul and to learn from him in life and ministry was an enormous privilege.

First and foremost, we are disciples of Jesus, our Saviour and Lord. We have heard his call to follow him and have understood that discipleship involves putting him before every other relationship, before personal interest and even before life itself (Luke 14:25–27). We have responded to Jesus because we love him and we truly desire to be like him. We have made it our life's ambition, by his grace, to serve him well and, for us, finding the pearl of great price – the kingdom of God – reset our compass. Now we have the Holy Spirit within – the source of life and love, who constantly seeks to draw us closer to the Father, to Jesus and to one another; teaching, guiding and empowering us.

The good news is we were never intended to make it on our own. This same Jesus, who is Saviour and Lord, has made provision for us to receive encouragement and help towards the goal, through discipleship within the body of Christ – a community of fellow disciples. Those who are farther along the road can show us the way as we in turn, one day, will be able to train others. Taking on board what Jesus said, it actually gets quite personal because, if I am going to be truly discipled, I will need to be willing for someone else to speak into my life. I will need to be open with someone who can help me to grow into the image of Jesus. And that raises all sorts of healthy questions about the nature of such a discipling relationship, which we will explore.

Take Peter – an apprentice who became an apostle

The best way to begin is to look at how Jesus did it. His way of discipling the twelve was to be their example of discipling others, as they went out to fulfil his commission, and it is ours too. We are going to follow the journey of just one of them, from his very first meeting with Jesus to the day he was 'airborne' in the power of the Spirit at Pentecost. Whether we are being discipled, or discipling others, or both, the story is full of lessons; and I think we will see that to be truly discipled is a huge privilege and wholly a blessing. Then, once we have built a picture of what it means in practice in Part One, we will explore the nature of a church community in which discipleship can flourish in Part Two.

We love Peter because of his human frailty – the impulsiveness, the enthusiasm, the flaws, all mixed up together. He was so like us. Always sticking his head above the parapet and occasionally getting it shot off. He lived up at the top end of the country and spoke Aramaic with a northern accent. He was born in a lakeside town, married and a bit of an entrepreneur; he part-owned a fishing business with two friends. I think what you saw was what you got! He was a loveable hothead, whose heart was basically in the right place.

So how do you go about training someone like Peter in this new way of life? Where do you begin? How do you know you are succeeding? As we trace the answers, perhaps we may be challenged to take stock of how discipleship is working out in our own lives and in our churches. Jesus gives us a Masterclass.

For the eleven disciples, the commission they received from Jesus at that meeting in Galilee would shape the rest of their lives.

Meet me in Galilee – *reflections*

- What is your initial response to the concept of being personally discipled? Which words fit your feelings about it best, and why?
    - Uncertainty
    - Opportunity
    - Apprehension
    - Welcome
    - Noncommittal
    - Privilege

- Have you had previous experience of being discipled in some way, or of discipling others? If so, how do you look back on it now?

- Jesus' invitation is our starting point. He calls us to put him before every other relationship or personal interest. Take time to reflect on the implications. If the Holy Spirit is already reminding you of an existing challenge, why not ask the Lord to help you open your heart to him?

[1] *The Message* words this sentence like this: 'Some, though, held back, not sure about *worship*, about risking themselves totally'.
[2] Philip Vogel, *Go and Make Apprentices* (Kingsway, 1986) p26.
[3] Donald Hagner, *Matthew 14–28, Word Biblical Commentary* (Thomas Nelson, 1995) p887.

Chapter Two
Early days

Jesus believed in Peter and saw his potential

Andrew, his brother Simon, and Philip had come south. They were all from Bethsaida on the northern shore of the Sea of Galilee. Nathanael was down in Judea, too, but he was from the village of Cana, west of the lake. How many other Galileans had their curiosity aroused by the stories circulating about John the Baptist, we do not know. But when Andrew and a friend heard John preaching by the River Jordan, they were so stirred by his message that they became his disciples. They were both with him the day Jesus came walking by.

> *The next day John was there again with two of his disciples. When he saw Jesus passing by, he said, 'Look, the Lamb of God!' When the two disciples heard him say this, they followed Jesus … Andrew, Simon Peter's brother, was one of the two who heard what John had said and who had followed Jesus. The first thing Andrew did was to find his brother Simon and tell him, 'We have found the Messiah' (that is, the Christ). And he brought him to Jesus.*
>
> **(John 1:35–37,40–42)**

The two disciples of John transferred their focus from the prophet and forerunner to the One he spoke of. First thing next morning, Andrew is off to find his brother, Simon. 'We have found the Messiah!' he announces enthusiastically in John 1:41, and brings him to Jesus, hoping that his brother too will be persuaded. And so they meet – Jesus and Simon, face to face for the first time, looking each other in the eye.

*Jesus looked at him and said, 'You are Simon son of John.
You will be called Cephas' (which, when translated, is Peter).*

(John 1:42)

It means 'a rock'. I can imagine Andrew thinking to himself, 'Jesus, I think you might have just blown it. You are supposed to be the Messiah; you are talking to the most unpredictable, volatile man in Galilee, and you just called him *a rock!*' What Jesus was actually saying, was: 'Peter, I can see what you are going to be and I believe in you'. From the beginning, Jesus saw in the Galilean fisherman a foundational figure in the new community yet to emerge. Peter's first experience of Jesus was a greeting which was affirming and significant.

If someone is going to disciple me, I need to know that they believe in me, and that they have a vision for what I could be. I have had the privilege of having just such a person in my life since my early thirties, who has stood with me and discipled me over the years. When we met in the early seventies, John Noble was a father figure in the growing house church movement in the United Kingdom. Forty years later I still count it a privilege to call him my friend. I cannot tell you how much I have learned from his example and his wise counsel, always offered honestly, but with love and encouragement. And I am aware that, like me, many have been influenced at a deeply personal level.

There was a point, some twenty-five years ago, when my ministry was that close to extinction that David Attenborough was attending with a cameraman. But John never stopped believing in me. He never lost touch or gave up, even though at the time Muriel and I were living three hundred miles away. And through his encouragement and faithfulness, new lessons were learned and new doors began to open, which actually led on to the most fruitful twenty years of my life (so far!). I think Timothy experienced the same kind of affirmation and shaping from Paul.

Jesus believed in Peter and had a vision for what he could be. It is an essential ingredient in any discipling relationship.

Jesus showed Peter what it is like to live under the anointing

The day after his first meeting with Peter, Jesus decided to leave for Galilee (John 1:43). Perhaps they had already received an invitation to the upcoming wedding at Cana. Andrew and Peter, Philip and Nathanael go with him. Luke takes up the story.

> *Jesus returned to Galilee in the power of the Spirit, and news about him spread through the whole countryside.*
>
> **(Luke 4:14)**

When Jesus arrived back in Galilee, it was soon evident that something dramatic had happened to him while he was away. At his baptism in the Jordan, he had been anointed with the Holy Spirit and empowered for mission. On his return to Galilee, miracles began to happen, first at the wedding, then at Capernaum. The Spirit's power could be seen. At the end of Luke 4, we learn that Peter has moved from Bethsaida to Capernaum and Jesus is now in his home, healing Peter's mother-in-law of a high fever. In Luke 5, Jesus is preaching to a large crowd by the Sea of Galilee.

> *One day as Jesus was standing by the Lake of Gennesaret, the people were crowding round him and listening to the word of God. He saw at the water's edge two boats, left there by the fishermen, who were washing their nets. He got into one of the boats, the one belonging to Simon, and asked him to put out a little from shore. Then he sat down and taught the people from the boat. When he had finished speaking, he said to Simon, 'Put out into deep water, and let down the nets for a catch.' Simon answered, 'Master, we've worked hard all night and haven't caught anything. But because you say so, I will let down the nets.' When they had done so, they caught*

such a large number of fish that their nets began to break.
So they signalled to their partners in the other boat to come
and help them, and they came and filled both boats so full
that they began to sink. When Simon Peter saw this, he fell at
Jesus' knees and said, 'Go away from me, Lord; I am a sinful
man!' For he and all his companions were astonished at the
catch of fish they had taken, and so were James and John,
the sons of Zebedee, Simon's partners.

(Luke 5:1–10a)

Filled with the Holy Spirit, Jesus is living his life in the will of the Father, and that is what Peter is seeing. In effect, Jesus is saying, 'Peter, this is what it's like, living under the anointing of the Spirit'.

If I am discipling someone else, that's quite a challenge! Can they see in me what it's like to be living in the power of the Holy Spirit? Can they see the fruit of his presence in my life? However good our teaching, at the end of the day we *are* our ministry and that is what we will communicate. Our own relationship with God is at the core of what we impart. Discipling others is more about example than information.

It has been said before, but it really does come down to a simple, extraordinarily challenging question: 'Who wants your life?' Which is not to say, your car, your house, your job prospects – life doesn't consist in those things. Who wants your real life? At the end of the day we can only lead others where we have been. Those twenty-seven named people who were invited to accompany Paul seized the opportunity, even if it meant travelling long months with the apostle, accepting the risks of sharing a prison cell with him or getting caught up in one of his fairly regular beatings. And they did it because of the value they placed upon his relationship with the Lord and his experience of the Spirit in life and ministry. The Holy Spirit was forming and directing those significant relationships between Paul and his companions, and the repercussions would spread across the growing Gentile churches.

Dan Kimball records a personal experience in his challenging book, *The Emerging Church: Vintage Christianity for New Generations.* Writing in a chapter about spiritual formation, he says:

> *God placed Dr. John Mitchell in my life. I had the privilege*
> *of meeting with him almost weekly while I was a student*
> *at Multnomah Biblical Seminary in Portland, Oregon.*
> *Quite honestly, I didn't think his teaching was riveting, but*
> *I found that sitting in his office listening to him pray was*
> *a life-changing experience. The advice and wisdom of Dr.*
> *Mitchell, who was over ninety when I met him, left an indelible*
> *impression. Seeing his love for the Scriptures inspired me far*
> *beyond any sermon ever could and instilled in me a love of God's*
> *Word that remains to this day. His intimate walk with Jesus*
> *was something I can only explain as being truly supernatural.*[1]

Jesus showed Peter how to live under the anointing of the Spirit.

Jesus prophesied over his life

Following the miracle of the catch of fish, Jesus has something to say to Peter about things to come: 'Then Jesus said to Simon, "Don't be afraid; from now on you will fish for people"' (Luke 5:10b).

At this early stage, Jesus has heard God for Peter. He is helping him to identify his gifting and encouraging him into his future. God's purpose for Peter was that he should be not only a rock upon whom others would rely, but someone who would see large numbers of people coming into the kingdom. He would be as successful in proclaiming Jesus and calling men and women to respond to his Lordship, as he was (when Jesus got involved) at filling the boat with fish that night. Part of Jesus' input into Peter, prompted by the Spirit, was to help him hear God about the shape of things to come.

One of the aims of discipleship is to help someone learn how to connect with God's voice and his purpose for their life. Knowing who I am and what God has called me to do is key to growing up in Christ and fulfilling my potential as a person and as a servant of the Lord Jesus. Loving myself as I love my neighbour and finding my place in the body of Christ opens the door to a future of fulfilment and fruitfulness, and connects me with my God-given calling. Peterson put it this way in *The Message*: 'It's in Christ that we find out who we are and what we are living for. Long before we first heard of Christ and got our hopes up, he had his eye on us, had designs on us for glorious living, part of the overall purpose he is working out in everything and everyone' (Eph. 1:11).

Again, we don't have to work it all out alone and struggle to make something happen – help is at hand! It's called discipleship, which can be found in relationship with a community of disciples. I am grateful to those who spoke into my life, particularly at formative stages, but also along the way, helping me to discover who I am and where the grace of God was pointing in my life. Peter would yet have to learn that his personal place in the kingdom was bound up with his fellow disciples, but Jesus would come to that later. One step at a time! For now, it was about getting him on track. And Peter responded to what he heard – he was going for it.

....

Early days – *reflections*

Being discipled

- Have you known someone in your Christian life who has believed in you through the highs and lows? What did it mean to you?

- How would you respond if you had an opportunity to be consistently discipled by someone who was affirming and enthusiastic about how God wanted to equip you and use you in the future?

- Are you clear about what is your main area of gifting – and the calling in which God might want you to serve him? If so, can you sum it up succinctly?

- If prophetic words have been spoken over you about your life and calling, what steps could you take towards being ready for those words to be fulfilled? How could you seek God more proactively about what he has said?

Discipling others

- Think about what you most want God to give you for others. Then tell him – you might be surprised by how much you are blessed!

- If Jesus was to talk to you about how you disciple others, what might he want to address?

- When you think about your own life as an example to others, are there areas which give you concern? If there are, what do you think the Lord would like you to do, in order to move forward?

[1] Dan Kimball, *The Emerging Church: Vintage Christianity for New Generations* (Zondervan, 2003) pp218–219.

Chapter Three
Learning and growing

Peter became one of Jesus' closest friends

The first time I realised that my brother, Brian, was developing a romantic relationship with a certain young lady (who later became his wife) was when I saw Ruth run up to him and say, 'I've got loads of things to tell you'.

The evening before he died, Jesus said something very special to the Eleven: 'Now you are my friends, since I have told you everything the Father told me' (John 15:15, NLT).

Peter, James and John were especially close to Jesus. They were the three who were invited into quite intimate situations, such as the healing of Jairus' daughter, or the exquisite moment on the mountain when Jesus was transfigured. What Peter saw that day he never forgot, recalling some thirty-five years later how Jesus received 'honour and glory from God the Father when the voice came to him from the Majestic Glory' (2 Pet. 1:17). And it was in Gethsemane, at the moment of intense human need, that Jesus sought the company of Peter, James and John – his closest friends.

Discipleship was taking place in the context of a personal relationship. It was not a Western classroom model of learning, but the Jewish model – the way Paul had been 'brought up ... under Gamaliel' (Acts 22:3), to whom he would have attached himself for the purpose of learning from him.

There was openness between Jesus and Peter and an appreciation of each other. It was a relationship of trust – so essential if discipleship is going to be a blessing and fruitful. Life's experiences were shared. Mark describes how Jesus called his twelve disciples: 'He appointed twelve *that they might be with him* and that he might send them out'

(Mark 3:14, italics mine). These were the twelve whom Jesus chose to train personally; they were invited to spend time with him; they ate together and travelled together; they were able to share his difficult days as well as the exhilarating days.

It was *being* together and *doing* things together. That is discipleship at its best and at its most effective. It can happen in the stuff of life, in the ebb and flow of opportunity and challenge. When it comes to training leaders it is surely an indispensable element. In Part Two we will explore the nature of committed relationships in the body of Christ, because discipleship of this sort can only take place in a context of love and faithfulness.

Peter displayed the spirit of a disciple

It is remarkable how often we find Peter asking questions:

> *Jesus called the crowd to him and said, 'Listen and understand. What goes into someone's mouth does not defile them, but what comes out of their mouth, that is what defiles them.' … Peter said, 'Explain the parable to us.'*
>
> **(Matt. 15:10–11,15)**

> *On their arrival in Capernaum, the collectors of the Temple tax came to Peter and asked him, 'Doesn't your teacher pay the Temple tax?' 'Yes, he does,' Peter replied. Then he went into the house. But before he had a chance to speak, Jesus asked him …*
>
> **(Matt. 17:24, NLT)**

> *Then Peter came to Jesus and asked, 'Lord, how many times shall I forgive my brother or sister who sins against me? Up to seven times?'*
>
> **(Matt. 18:21)**

*'But understand this: if the owner of the house had known
at what hour the thief was coming, he would not have let his
house be broken into. You also must be ready, because the Son
of Man will come at an hour when you do not expect him.' Peter
asked, 'Lord, are you telling this parable to us, or to everyone?'*

(Luke 12:39–41)

*'My children, I will be with you only a little longer. You will
look for me, and just as I told the Jews, so I tell you now:
where I am going, you cannot come.' ... Simon Peter asked
him, 'Lord, where are you going?'*

(John 13:33,36)

Peter was constantly asking questions of Jesus because he was hungry to learn and to understand. The direction of his life had changed – discipleship had become a priority. He was pressing in, taking initiative as well as responding to the things Jesus did and said. In Jesus' own words, Peter was *'seek[ing] first* [God's] kingdom and his righteousness' (Matt. 6:33, italics mine). This was more than his natural enthusiasm showing itself – Peter had the spirit of a true disciple.

We see the same spirit when the disciples were alone in the boat just before dawn, about three or four miles out, pounded by the waves and straining at the oars. The sight of Jesus walking on the water terrifies them at first, but hearing his voice, Peter calls out, 'Lord, if it's you ... tell me to come to you on the water' (Matt. 14:28). He's leaning over the edge, ready to go. 'Is it OK if I jump?' He gets the go-ahead and, despite a wobble and a rescue grab, makes it to Jesus. The same abandon prompted Peter's response to Jesus' question after many of His disciples gave up.

*After this a lot of his disciples left. They no longer wanted to be
associated with him. Then Jesus gave the Twelve their chance:
'Do you also want to leave?' Peter replied, 'Master, to whom*

would we go? You have the words of real life, eternal life. We've already committed ourselves, confident that you are the Holy One of God.'

(John 6:67–68, *The Message*)

Discipleship will be most fruitful in our lives when we display the same spirit. I mentioned earlier how my own life has been influenced by the faithful care and input of John Noble. Thinking back to the early days, when I needed to learn even more than I do now (if that's possible!), I was happy to make the 280-mile round trip from Bristol to Romford, because I was keen to seek John's wisdom. Similarly, Muriel and I would have time with John and Christine together, either in their home or ours, and they were able to help us, both in our marriage and in our ministry. Proverbs 20:5 (NLT, 1996) sums it up: 'Though good advice lies deep within a person's heart, the wise will draw it out.'

When I have had the privilege of discipling others, it has always been most fruitful (and most rewarding) when they have run with the ball, demonstrating the eagerness that was so characteristic of Peter. It brings out the best. True discipleship will always be marked by enthusiasm and a readiness to listen and consider. Peter grew more quickly because of the spirit he displayed.

Equally important is the spirit in which discipleship is offered. We are all disciples of Jesus first and as such, our place is at his feet together in worship and gratitude for his incredible grace. When instruction and counsel are offered to another it can only be with humility; always honouring those who are wanting to learn and grow, always respecting their personal integrity, their responsibility for their own relationship with Jesus and their freedom of choice and action. Wise disciples will watch closely, listen well and weigh carefully, but ultimately the responsibility for their walk with the Lord is theirs alone. But more of that in Part Two.

Jesus taught the disciples as a group

Jesus understood the importance of developing not only his disciples' personal character and ministry, but also their understanding. Moving from an age of law to the age of the Spirit; from the traditions of the elders to the freedoms of grace; from temple to living temple; from animal sacrifices and priesthood to the victorious sacrifice of Jesus and priestly access for all; from a kingdom that seemed distant to a kingdom which was also here and now – there was so much to learn. Teaching was vital and Jesus did this with the group as a whole. Many times he withdrew with his disciples or taught them by the way, or explained to them privately the meaning of what had been said in public. Mark 9:30–31 is just such an occasion: 'They left that place and passed through Galilee. Jesus did not want anyone to know where they were, because he was teaching his disciples.'

The introduction to what is called The Sermon on the Mount points to something similar: 'Now when Jesus saw the crowds, he went up on a mountainside and sat down. His disciples came to him, and he began to teach them' (Matt. 5:1–2). We have already noted Peterson's translation: 'When Jesus saw his ministry drawing huge crowds, he climbed a hillside. Those who were apprenticed to him, the committed, climbed with him. Arriving at a quiet place, he sat down and taught his climbing companions.'

It appears that Jesus withdrew to find a quiet place to teach his disciples, even if, as the end of Matthew 7 suggests, the crowds gathered round before he had finished. It isn't that Jesus was unmindful of the crowds – he truly *saw* them. He would return to the crowds later and continue proclaiming and demonstrating the good news, and the men he was training would shortly be sent out across Galilee and, ultimately, far and wide. Investment in the few was for the sake of the many.

Over the period of his ministry, Jesus taught the disciples many things. He spoke about the kingdom of God, its nature, its values and its growth; he spoke of the Father's heart, about grace and forgiveness for prodigals and the difference between religion and relationship with God; he talked about eternal life and the Spirit within; about light and darkness, love and relationships; about prayer and justice, especially for the poor; he taught them that the real enemy was not the occupying Roman army but Satan, 'the ruler of this world' (mentioned three times in John's Gospel – John 12:31, 14:30, 16:11, NRSV), who had usurped authority over the earth but would be defeated when the Son of Man was 'lifted up'. So much to teach them, so little time, but the Holy Spirit would continue the task when Jesus was no longer with them.

Corporate teaching and personal discipleship belong together. Teaching on its own is insufficient; discipleship without understanding is dangerous. When teaching and discipleship complement each other we are faced with practical issues, and help is at hand as we seek to live out what we learn. Discipleship offers a reality check. It stimulates us to ask ourselves: 'Is what I am hearing becoming part of my life? Am I being informed or transformed?'

No one was more closely connected to reality than Jesus, or more gracious in helping his disciples to embrace it.

....

Learning and growing – *reflections*

Being discipled

- Despite his faults, Peter displayed the spirit of a disciple. On the following scale, where would you place your approach to discipleship?

  – Radical pursuit

  – Measured commitment

  – Fitting it in to a busy life when you can

  – Reluctant involvement

  – Not happening

- What would you like to see change? Ask God to speak to you about it.

- Does great Bible teaching leave you satisfied and fulfilled, or passionate about change in your life? Think about that. What did you feel when you read the words: 'Am I being informed or transformed?'

Discipling others

- How, in practice, do you see the relationship between discipleship and friendship?

- What are the challenges of working closely with a disciple? In what ways does your approach express humility, honour and respect?

- What was your response to the conclusion: 'Corporate teaching and personal discipleship belong together. Teaching on its own is insufficient; discipleship without understanding is dangerous'?

Chapter Four
Stepping out

Jesus sent Peter out (as part of a team) to do what he had seen Jesus doing

As Jesus' ministry spread across Galilee and beyond, Peter and the other disciples saw him performing many miracles. They heard astonishing words about the kingdom of God being 'near' (Matt. 4:17), 'at hand' (NASB), 'right on your doorstep' (Luke 10:9, *The Message*). And they witnessed a new kind of authority, both in teaching and in casting out demons, such as no one else possessed. Jesus frequently took them aside to explain more, to help them understand the hidden meaning of powerful images.

At this stage they could hardly have grasped the purpose of this concentrated period of training, but they were being equipped to be his ambassadors after his return to the Father. And now it was time for them to step out without Jesus taking the public lead.

> When Jesus had called the Twelve together, he gave them
> power and authority to drive out all demons and to cure
> diseases, and he sent them out to proclaim the kingdom of
> God and to heal those who were ill … So they set out and
> went from village to village, proclaiming the good news and
> healing people everywhere.
>
> (Luke 9:1–2,6)

Jesus is developing both Peter's character and his ministry. Now Peter gets the chance to spread his wings a little, the opportunity to do what he has watched Jesus doing. He will be taking wobbly steps of faith; not alone, but side-by-side with another member of the Twelve as they were sent out in twos. Jesus' entire approach to discipling them demonstrated his wisdom and care for each one, as well as his strategy.

The disciples can hardly believe their success as they travel the countryside, doing what, until then, only Jesus had done. The sending out of the Twelve across the region of Galilee was an extension of Jesus' personal ministry and such was the combined impact that Herod Antipas, who was in charge of Galilee, 'heard about all that was going on' (Luke 9:7). His patch was echoing all over with talk of miracles and of a kingdom that clearly wasn't Caesar's and certainly wasn't his!

The lesson is simple. The best way to develop in ministry is first to be alongside someone who is farther along the road in the same area of gifting. Suppose, for example, I had an ability to connect with people, a burden for the lost that lived with me all the time, and the stirrings of an evangelistic heart; can I spend time with someone who is seasoned in winning others to Christ? Can I watch them doing it and work with them as I learn, before launching out in a wider sphere? We notice a young Christian who has the seeds of a prophetic calling; there is early evidence of meaningful words being given, with blessing and fruit. How can we facilitate the teaming up of that fledgling gift with someone who is more experienced in hearing God and prophesying, in a context of fellowship and accountability?

It's the difference between, on the one hand, being exhorted from the platform about the need to pray more (which is always undeniable) and, on the other hand, being asked by someone who has learned to live in the presence of God, 'How would you like to pray with me each week?' In developing any area of gift, biblical teaching is important and needed, but personal discipleship brings a dimension of growth and development which up-front teaching alone can never achieve. Imagine the resources that could be released in the body of Christ if we were able to facilitate the development of every single member of the body into their full potential for the kingdom!

The wonderful thing about Peter's experience of being discipled was that Jesus was willing to take risks. Peter was sent out in Jesus' name, but how would he represent the Master? Would the impetuous Peter get it 'right'? Would he mess up? Would he misrepresent the message of Jesus, or the spirit of it? Jesus sent him out in his own name because he was willing to stand by him if he made mistakes. In true discipleship there is room to breathe and grow, and reassurance and safety as you do so. There are opportunities to take bigger steps of faith in a safe environment, knowing that we are loved and cared for and that we will be supported through thick and thin.

Jesus gave them time for feedback

Going from village to village in pairs, the Twelve proclaimed the good news of the kingdom and called people to repentance. They demonstrated the kingdom by healing 'many people who were ill' and driving out 'many demons' (Mark 6:13). Returning from their travels they couldn't wait to find Jesus and tell him all about it.

> *When the apostles returned, they reported to Jesus what they had done. Then he took them with him and they withdrew by themselves to a town called Bethsaida*
>
> **(Luke 9:10)**

Jesus knew the importance of talking through their experiences – the highs and the lows, the lessons learned, perhaps the questions they hadn't been able to answer. He made time to be with them in a quiet place (at least until their privacy was invaded by the crowds again). Jesus gave them space for review and support. There was accountability. Everywhere we look in the story of Jesus' relationship with Peter and the other disciples we find important lessons for ourselves.

Not only could they benefit from the joy and blessing of recounting their stories, receiving approval and encouragement, but Jesus could bring adjustment where necessary, or new insights into the situations they had come across. Rather than being let off as loose cannons, the disciples had the security and blessing of being accountable, allowing their faith and confidence to grow. It is a comprehensive example of what discipleship is meant to be.

Leaders in diverse areas of church life and mission are always facing the dilemma of prioritising the use of precious time. Confronted by the enormity of the need and the challenge of meeting those needs, it is so easy to devote our diaries to activities that address the immediate. Jesus knew that although the fields were ripe for harvest, the key to the long-term growth of the kingdom was for him to step back regularly and invest time in his disciples. A 'thought-for-thought' translation of Mark 9:30–31 has it this way: 'Jesus didn't want anyone to know he was there, for he wanted to spend more time with his disciples and teach them' (NLT). Sensitive to the Spirit's guidance, Jesus guarded quality time with those on whom the future would depend.

Peter receives revelation for himself

Jesus and his disciples arrive at Caesarea Philippi, a beautiful location to the north of the Sea of Galilee, in sight of Mount Hermon. He asks them a question:

> When Jesus came to the region of Caesarea Philippi, he asked
> his disciples, 'Who do people say the Son of Man is?' They
> replied, 'Some say John the Baptist; others say Elijah; and
> still others, Jeremiah or one of the prophets.' 'But what about
> you?' he asked. 'Who do you say I am?' Simon Peter answered,
> 'You are the Messiah, the Son of the living God.' Jesus replied,
> 'Blessed are you, Simon son of Jonah, for this was not revealed
> to you by flesh and blood, but by my Father in heaven.
>
> (Matt. 16:13–17)

What is happening here? It is, of course, a remarkable confession of faith, declaring who Jesus of Nazareth really is, but in the light of Peter's journey it represents another step forward. Peter is now receiving revelation for himself. Whereas at the beginning we noted that Jesus was hearing God for Peter, now Peter is hearing God directly: 'this was … revealed to you … by my Father in heaven'. Peter is growing!

Another important principle emerges. The purpose of discipleship is not to make or keep one person dependent on another, but to help them grow in their own experience of God. It is to enable them to become more mature, able to live life out of their own relationship with the Father; better able to recognise his voice, to understand his purposes and to become more fruitful. So, for example, my relationship with John has evolved over the years. With the passing of time came a growing sense of areas where we might complement and bless each other. I still greatly appreciate the fact that his wise counsel is available, should I wish to draw on it, but hopefully discipleship has led to an increased maturity.

Often, an opportunity for discipleship will be more short term, sometimes defined in advance. But always the goal will be the same – the development and maturity of the disciple, equipping them to function with greater assurance as they grow in their own experience of the Spirit's leading and enabling.

Peter is promised keys

Following Peter's declaration, 'You are the Messiah, the Son of the living God', Jesus has more to say to him about his future:

> *I will give you the keys of the kingdom of heaven; whatever*
> *you bind on earth will be bound in heaven, and whatever you*
> *loose on earth will be loosed in heaven.*

> **(Matt. 16:19)**

Peter has displayed the spirit of a disciple, seeking to learn and understand. He has been growing day by day in experiences of faith and revelation. Now he hears that he is to be invested with a very special spiritual authority – 'the keys of the kingdom'. (The idea appears to stem from Isaiah 22:20–22, where Eliakim becomes the steward in charge of the palace and is given authority: 'the key to the house of David'.)

The first exercise of Peter's stewardship would come on the Day of Pentecost, when Peter proclaimed the resurrection and Lordship of Jesus and held open the door of the kingdom to the Jews in Jerusalem. But perhaps the most dramatic use of the keys in the Early Church would occur later, in Acts 10, when he would receive a revelation that would rock the Early Jewish Church to its foundations. First the vision of the sheet let down from heaven, containing all kinds of animals, 'clean' and 'unclean'; then 'a voice' – a voice he had learned to recognise. Then, travelling obediently from Joppa to the house of the centurion at Caesarea, Peter would preach the Lordship of Jesus over 'all' – Jew and Gentile – and witness a stunning event as the Spirit was poured out upon a Roman centurion and his relatives and friends. As a result he would lead the Jerusalem church into the era-changing revelation that 'even to Gentiles God has granted repentance that leads to life' (Acts 11:18).

When Peter first heard the words 'I will give you the keys' from Jesus, he could not have imagined how much it meant or what was to come. All of that was a long way down the road from this moment in Caesarea Philippi and from Peter's present journey. Even after his bold confession of faith there were still painful lessons to come. But the disciple who asked lots of questions and pressed in to learn; who jumped out of the boat and walked before he wobbled; who learned to hear from the Father and never lost the spirit of a kingdom seeker – he was the one who was entrusted with the keys. Discipleship is the path to true spiritual authority.

Before we leave Caesarea Philippi, it is worth noting that Paul, the apostle to the Gentiles, walked through the door that Peter opened. After meeting with Jesus on the Damascus road, Saul of Tarsus, the high-powered academic who had been 'advancing in Judaism beyond many of [his] own age' (Gal. 1:14), is found sitting at the feet of a relatively unknown disciple called Ananias, finding out what to do next and receiving prayer. Like Peter, Paul also displayed the spirit of a disciple. And the rest is history.

....

Stepping out – *reflections*

Being discipled

- How would you regard the opportunity to get alongside someone who could guide and develop your growth in personal ministry (in whatever sphere)? Do you think it would:
    - Cramp your style?
    - Hold you back when you just want to get on with it?
    - Provide you with a foundation which would benefit you (and the kingdom) in the long term?
    - Test you in terms of being teachable, or able to take direction?
    - Offer you an invaluable opportunity to learn from another's experience?

- If you are not already in a fruitful, discipling relationship, why not talk to your church leaders about the possibilities?

- How are you growing in your ability to hear God speaking – either to you personally, or to you for someone else?

Discipling others

- How could you adjust your approach to personal ministry to include the personal training of one or more alongside you?

- Are there areas in your own ministry where gaps could be filled, or aspects could be strengthened, if you were more pro-active about receiving help and training, while continuing to invest in those who look to you?

- 'Discipleship is the path to true spiritual authority' – a thought to reflect on and discuss.

Chapter Five
Failure and restoration

When it was necessary Jesus gave clear correction

Opposition from the religious authorities had been evident for some time; now scheming is going on behind closed doors. From this point, the disciples hear Jesus saying things that seriously didn't make sense. Or so it seemed.

> *From that time on Jesus began to explain to his disciples that he must go to Jerusalem and suffer many things at the hands of the elders, the chief priests and the teachers of the law, and that he must be killed and on the third day be raised to life. Peter took him aside and began to rebuke him. 'Never, Lord!' he said. 'This shall never happen to you!' Jesus turned and said to Peter, 'Get behind me, Satan! You are a stumbling-block to me; you do not have in mind the concerns of God, but merely human concerns.'*
>
> (Matt. 16:21–23)

Jesus' announcement to the disciples came as a devastating blow and was totally incomprehensible. Suffering and death for the Messiah did not fit with their expectations. It appears that Jesus' promise about resurrection on the third day simply didn't make it through the mist of shock and disbelief about the prediction of his death. For the positive, all-or-nothing Peter, the whole concept was unthinkable and something had to be done quickly. His only concession to protocol was to take Jesus to one side before actually daring to *rebuke* the Master.

Faced with Peter's reaction and recognising behind his outburst the tempter's seductive tones, Jesus responds even more strongly: 'Get behind me, Satan! You are a stumbling-block to me; you do not have in mind the concerns of God, but merely human concerns.' Strong words indeed to a disciple who had earlier made such a remarkable confession of faith. Jesus didn't hold back from telling Peter what he needed to hear – he loved him far too much for that. There was honesty in the relationship. Peter was still learning the true nature of the kingdom of which he had become a part – he didn't yet understand that the path to exaltation lay through Gethsemane and the cross.

True discipleship involves honesty. Sometimes we need to give or receive faithful love. That is why openness is at the heart of meaningful discipleship. If there are eggshells on the pathway to my door, it's going to be pretty difficult for anyone to disciple me and, sadly, I am the one who will miss out.

I remember one occasion some years ago when I sought John's input regarding a particular role in ministry which I felt the Lord was indicating for me. After some weeks of reflection and dialogue John said things to me which I really, really didn't want to hear. I chose to honour his judgment, albeit through tears, but a few years later it became so clear that he had been right. As a result I needed to go to another friend in ministry to ask his forgiveness, which he freely gave. I am so glad that John was honest with me. It was faithful love.

In bringing correction to Peter, Jesus was neither blinded by talent nor inhibited by friendship. Indeed, it was that very friendship and love, undergirding their relationship, that enabled Jesus to bring Peter through the much deeper waters that lay ahead. In Part Two we will be looking at the nature of the kingdom of light, and the value and blessing of openness and honesty within the community of disciples.

Jesus warned Peter when he saw the danger signals

After Jesus' exchange with Peter, he talks to the Twelve about denying themselves and taking up the cross. The disciples' pathway, in their measure, would mirror his. Then he concludes by saying, 'Truly I tell you, some who are standing here will not taste death before they see the Son of Man coming in his kingdom' (Matt. 16:28). Not all of them, just 'some'.

The promise was fulfilled about a week later (Matthew thought it was six days, Luke reckoned it was eight). On the Mount of Transfiguration, Peter, James and John were privileged to become 'eye-witnesses of his majesty' (2 Pet. 1:16). The glory of that scene foreshadowed 'the coming of our Lord Jesus Christ in power' (2 Pet. 1:16) – Peter links the two events. But the three disciples also saw and heard Moses and Elijah talking with Jesus about his 'exodus' – his journey through suffering and death to victory over the unseen enemy and deliverance for his people. On the Mount of Transfiguration, heaven and earth came together to help Peter, James and John grasp what seemed impossible to reconcile – the glory, the power and the suffering to come.

And now the trek south begins. Jesus and his disciples set off from Caesarea Philippi, first to Galilee, then on towards Judea and, finally, to Jerusalem itself. The women who had travelled around Galilee, ministering to the needs of Jesus, go with them – all the way. Mary Magdalene, Joanna, Susanna, another Mary and others – their steadfast loyalty was a shining example to the men (they stood within sight of the cross when others had fled; they followed Joseph of Arimathea closely to see where Jesus' body was going to be buried, and they were back at the tomb first thing on Sunday morning – Luke 8:1–4; 23:49,55–56; 24:1). I think those courageous Galilean women, from different walks of life, were quite amazing disciples. Luke evidently thought so, too. The devoted followers of Jesus were not an all-male group.

Following the 'triumphal entry' and the events of that week, Luke leads us in his narrative to the upper room. Jesus is sitting with his disciples, eating the Passover meal. He has broken bread and shared wine with them. Judas has left. Incredibly, there has been a discussion about which of them is the greatest and now Jesus has something to say to Peter:

> Simon, Simon, Satan has asked to sift all of you as wheat.
> But I have prayed for you, Simon, that your faith may
> not fail. And when you have turned back, strengthen your
> brothers.
>
> **(Luke 22:31–32, TNIV)**

Jesus is saying, 'Peter, right now you are a target and you are in danger of coming a cropper'. In chapter 6:14 Luke had informed his readers that 'Peter' was the new name given by Jesus to Simon. Luke hasn't used Peter's original name since that point – until now, when it is spoken three times. Was the old Simon coming to the surface?

In Mark's record, Peter's reply included the bold claim that even if Jesus couldn't rely on the others, his own faithfulness was rock solid: 'Even if all fall away, I will not' (Mark 14:29). The other disciples appear to have said similar things, but somehow there is a prominence about Peter. Satan was indeed out to get them all, but Jesus prayed for Peter in particular because he saw in him a vulnerability that would be exposed during the testing times ahead.

Later that night in Gethsemane, Peter, James and John were all sleeping, but it is to Peter that Jesus spoke first: 'Simon ... are you asleep? Couldn't you keep watch for one hour?' Then to all three: 'Watch and pray so that you will not fall into temptation. The spirit is willing, but the flesh is weak' (Mark 14:37–38).

Have you ever looked back and thought – I wish someone could have warned me just then? Someone who had been looking out for me and was close enough to share their concern? Jesus could say what he did to Peter because the relationship was in place, though sadly, on this occasion, Peter's heart wasn't fully open to what he heard. Yet behind the warnings, Jesus was praying for him, because he cared for him and wanted him to succeed. That's the kind of person I want to disciple me!

Satan's designs on the group – and especially on Peter because he was the emerging leader – weren't simply to trip them up, but to undermine their faith in Jesus at a fundamental level. That is what Jesus prayed about and his prayer was answered. Peter's courage faltered under extraordinary fire, but through the heartbreak his faith emerged again. Like gold.

After Peter's fall Jesus saw him through to restoration

The Master signals it is time to go. He talks about the true vine, about his Father's love and his own love for them, and about the Holy Spirit he would send to help them understand. Then he stops and begins to pray (John 17). As we look over the disciples' shoulders we catch a glimpse of a wonderfully intimate moment between the Father and the Son, so close together as they approach the place of sacrifice: 'Father, the hour has come. Glorify your Son, that your Son may glorify you' (John 17:1). Each so caring for the other; each sharing an exquisite intimacy that was at the heart of the gathering storm. How much the Eleven must have learned about prayer in those moments! Discipleship is like that.

> *When he had finished praying, Jesus left with his disciples and*
> *crossed the Kidron Valley. On the other side there was a garden*
>
> **(John 18:1)**

In Gethsemane, Jesus seeks the company of the three disciples closest to him – Peter, James and John – as he enters into an agony of prayer in a scene which was more intimate and moving still. Then the ominous events begin to unfold.

Perhaps we should pause before rushing to castigate Peter for his part in what was to follow. When the soldiers and temple officers arrive to make the arrest, Jesus identifies himself and asks them to let his disciples go. In his earlier prayer (John 17:12), Jesus had told his Father, 'While I was with them, I protected them and kept them safe', and now, in the thick of it, the safety of his beloved disciples is still his chief concern.

> *Again he asked them, 'Who is it you want?' 'Jesus of Nazareth,' they said. Jesus answered, 'I told you that I am he. If you are looking for me, then let these men go.' This happened so that the words he had spoken would be fulfilled: 'I have not lost one of those you gave me.'*
>
> **(John 18:7–9)**

His request to the soldiers to let his friends go was tantamount to releasing the disciples from any pressure to stay and be captured, and they all slipped away. But it is a testimony to Peter's devoted response that he not only swung his sword at the High Priest's servant (however misguided), but was one of only two disciples who dared to track the arresting party back into the city. It was Peter's love for Jesus that put him in the hot spot in the first place. When Jesus looked out across the inner courtyard of Caiaphas' house and saw that Peter had got in, his disciple's commitment must surely have meant a great deal, even though Jesus had had to clean up after him by healing the servant's severed ear. It wasn't Jesus' style to harbour thoughts about his disciple's mistakes.

In the traumatic moments that followed, Peter faltered. The risk of being identified with the captive Jesus seemed momentarily overwhelming and Peter denied the Lord three times. It might have seemed unthinkable, given their amazing journey, but it happened. Sometimes the unthinkable does happen in the body of Christ. We all follow Jesus only by his grace.

*Just as he was speaking, the cock crowed. The Lord turned
and looked straight at Peter.*

(Luke 22:60–61)

Their eyes met, reminiscent of their very first meeting, three years
before. I don't think it was a condemning look – I think it was a look
that was full of compassion and love. One thing I know – it broke Peter's
heart. He went out and wept and wept and wept.

I can't imagine what the rest of the weekend was like for Peter:
the Master sentenced to death and crucified, the dream over, and
the last contact a moment of failure. Peter plumbed the depths of
disappointment with himself and confusion about Jesus. But then came
Sunday morning. Tradition as early as the second century consistently
agrees that Mark was a friend and associate of Peter and that Mark's
Gospel is his attempt to arrange and record the substance of Peter's
recollections and preaching. Not surprisingly, then, it is Mark who
tells us about the angel outside the empty tomb who had a very special
message. To the three women who had come just after sunrise to anoint
Jesus' body, the angel said, 'Don't be alarmed … You are looking for
Jesus the Nazarene, who was crucified. He has risen! He is not here. See
the place where they laid him. But go, tell his disciples *and Peter*, "He is
going ahead of you into Galilee. There you will see him, just as he told
you"' (Mark 16:6–7, italics mine).

Whatever you do, make sure you tell Peter! Jesus has only been
raised from the dead a few hours and he is back on the job already,
mindful of Peter. But that was only the beginning of grace and mercy
flowing like a river towards the fallen disciple. Paul describes the good
news: 'Christ died for our sins according to the Scriptures, that he was
buried, that he was raised on the third day according to the Scriptures,
and that *he appeared to Cephas* [Peter], and then to the Twelve'
(1 Cor. 15:3–5, italics mine). When Cleopas and the other disciple
rushed back from Emmaus to Jerusalem with their story of seeing Jesus
alive, the gathered disciples had already heard. 'It is true!' they said,

'The Lord has risen and has appeared to Simon' (Luke 24:34). Before Jesus revealed himself to the Eleven, he met Peter alone.

Who can imagine what passed between them? It was the moment of forgiveness, as Jesus wrapped his arms around a broken disciple. And Peter discovered the unbelievable – he hadn't shot his bolt with the Master. Fellowship was restored. Patiently, lovingly, truthfully, Jesus helped Peter to come through the experience of devastating failure and in so doing, gave a whole new meaning to the concept of making disciples.

Jesus addresses Peter's relationship with the other disciples

But there was one other area that needed the Master's attention and that was Peter's relationship with the others. He had taken a place beyond them all, asserting his personal loyalty, and there was going to be some repair work needed in the group as a whole. Jesus is as concerned about our relationships as he is about our personal growth and development.

In the last chapter of his Gospel, John records Jesus' third appearance to his disciples since his resurrection, this time by the Sea of Galilee. Seven of the disciples are together and decide to go fishing – that is to say, Peter decided and the others followed. They catch nothing all night and in the morning Jesus, at first unrecognised, is standing on the shore. On the instruction of the friendly stranger they let down the net and another miracle happens. One of the disciples recognises Jesus and whispers to Peter, 'It's the Lord!' Peter is over the side of the boat in a jiffy. No change there then! Soon they are enjoying a breakfast of fish and bread which Jesus had prepared for them and now he is ready to talk to Peter in front of the others:

> When they had finished eating, Jesus said to Simon Peter,
> 'Simon son of John, do you love me more than these?'

'Yes, Lord,' he said, 'you know that I love you.' Jesus said, 'Feed my lambs.' Again Jesus said, 'Simon son of John, do you love me?' He answered, 'Yes, Lord, you know that I love you.' Jesus said, 'Take care of my sheep.' The third time he said to him, 'Simon son of John, do you love me?'

(John 21:15–17)

Three times Jesus asked the question and John tells us, 'Peter was hurt' (John 21:17). It was a painful moment, but Jesus knew it was necessary. Finally, Peter blurts out, 'Lord, you know all things; you know that I love you' (John 21:17). Gently, Jesus restores Peter to his place among the disciples but with a new humility, and his call to leadership and ministry is reaffirmed: 'Take care of my sheep.' Jesus' example of leading Peter through to restoration included addressing his relationship with his brothers and sisters. Now there would be no undercurrents, no unspoken questions; they would be a united team, able to work together.

But there is one more exchange between them, which shows both Jesus' confidence in Peter for the future and Peter's constant need of keeping his eyes on the Master.

'Very truly I tell you, when you were younger you dressed yourself and went where you wanted; but when you are old you will stretch out your hands, and someone else will dress you and lead you where you do not want to go.' Jesus said this to indicate the kind of death by which Peter would glorify God.

(John 21:18–19)

Jesus indicates to Peter that he would suffer martyrdom, which is a fairly momentous, not to say sobering, word for anyone to receive. But looking back from our vantage point of having the book of Revelation before us, it is also significant. Martyrs are seen as victorious; they have followed the Lamb through death and have a place before the throne of God where they are cared for by the Eternal Shepherd. Jesus' prophetic words to Peter show that he anticipates his servant's steadfast faithfulness to the end. *He still believes in him* and he concludes by saying, 'Follow me!' (John 21:19).

Moments later, Peter looks around and sees 'the disciple whom Jesus loved' (John 21:20) – thought by many to be John. Without stopping to think he blurts out: 'what about him?' (John 21:21). Once more, it seems, Peter can't resist comparing himself with other disciples and Jesus has to remind him that such things are not his concern. John's future was between John and Jesus, and he repeats his call: 'You must follow me' (John 21:22).

The Master's restoring grace goes on and on, and so does his commitment to relational integrity.

Failure and restoration – *reflections*

Being discipled

- Accepting correction is a challenge for us all. If you were assessing your ability to receive corrective input, where would you place yourself on a scale of 1 – 10, where 10 is 'I normally welcome valid correction because I want to learn and grow' and 1 is, 'No chance!'?

- Peter's overconfidence led to him not really listening to Jesus' warnings, and left him vulnerable. Is there anything which might leave you open to enemy attack? If the Lord brings something to mind, ask him to show you how best to deal with it.

- After his fall, Peter learned that his failure hadn't affected the Master's love and commitment. If a mistake or failure from the past still casts a shadow over your relationship with Jesus and with others, what is Jesus saying to you now?

- Is there a dream or an aspiration which you gave up because you felt you had missed the way, but which you need to bring back to the feet of Jesus for *his* thoughts about it?

- Looking back, what experiences of victory in your own life bless and encourage you most?

Discipling others

- How do you deal with the challenge of speaking honestly to those you disciple, when there is an issue they appear to be avoiding? Would you be more likely to err on the side of remaining silent, so as to avoid the possibility of hurt or offence, or could you come across as over critical?

- How do you feel about being open enough to share your own experience of failure and restoration, as a way of identifying with and encouraging others?

- How do you enable others to feel secure in knowing that you love and care for them, and that you will be there for them, whatever?

Chapter Six
The anointed servant

Peter fulfils his destiny

In John's account, Jesus' first meeting with the disciples after rising from the dead was in Jerusalem that evening.

> On the evening of that first day of the week, when the
> disciples were together, with the doors locked for fear of the
> Jewish leaders, Jesus came and stood among them and said,
> 'Peace be with you!' After he said this, he showed them his
> hands and side. The disciples were overjoyed when they saw
> the Lord. Again Jesus said, 'Peace be with you! As the Father
> has sent me, I am sending you.' And with that he breathed on
> them and said, 'Receive the Holy Spirit.'
>
> **(John 20:19–22)**

I think that meant (loosely translated!), 'Now it's your turn!' Given that Luke records Jesus saying later, 'Do not leave Jerusalem, but wait for the gift my Father promised, which you have heard me speak about' (Acts 1:4), it would appear that Jesus' act was prophetic – living, powerful words that would be fulfilled a few weeks later at Pentecost. That is certainly when dramatic evidence accompanied the outpouring.

> When the day of Pentecost came, they were all together in
> one place. Suddenly a sound like the blowing of a violent
> wind came from heaven and filled the whole house where
> they were sitting. They saw what seemed to be tongues of fire
> that separated and came to rest on each of them. All of them

were filled with the Holy Spirit and began to speak in other tongues as the Spirit enabled them. Now there were staying in Jerusalem God-fearing Jews from every nation under heaven … Then Peter stood up with the Eleven, raised his voice and addressed the crowd

(Acts 2:1–5,14)

On the Day of Pentecost a restored Peter, empowered by the Spirit, stands up *with the Eleven* – that sounds better! – and begins to fulfil the destiny Jesus foresaw and prophesied for him three years before. And as he boldly proclaims the risen Lord, three thousand people respond to the Lordship of Jesus. Now he, too, is beginning to live and serve under the anointing of the Spirit. The servant had become a little more like the Master – he had been 'discipled'. Discipleship and anointing complement one another.

In his second recorded address to the Jerusalem crowds, after the healing of the crippled man at the temple gate, Peter says something which seems quite remarkable: 'You disowned the Holy and Righteous One and asked that a murderer be released to you' (Acts 3:14). I think if I had been there I might have said, 'Hang on a minute, Peter – *you* disowned him! And after all you have heard and seen!' The truth is that Peter had been led into such a place of forgiveness that he was free in his spirit to stand and deliver the Lord's message. That was real restoration! Peter is a wonderful example of a servant of Jesus 'ransomed, healed, restored, forgiven' – and fruitful. Discipleship had achieved the goal that Jesus had in mind from the beginning. The anointing of the Spirit had empowered a servant who was ready.

The story of the anointed servant goes on. Peter and John spent that night in jail and the next morning they are hauled before the Sanhedrin. Speaking in the presence of Annas and Caiaphas (in whose courtyard Peter had denied the Lord), Peter and John say, 'we cannot help speaking about what we have seen and heard' (Acts 4:20). That sounds like a new Peter. Not long after, they suffered the first flogging because 'they never stopped teaching and proclaiming the good news that Jesus is the Messiah' (Acts 5:42).

In Jerusalem people brought their sick people on to the streets so that Peter's shadow might fall across them. The crowds living in surrounding towns brought their sick and demon-tormented into the city. All of them were healed. The miracles performed by Jesus in the power of the Spirit are now being performed by Peter, in the power of the same Spirit. In Joppa, in the home of Dorcas, Peter 'got down on his knees and prayed' and the devout seamstress was raised from the dead (Acts 9:40). And it was the ground-breaking courage of Peter which led to the momentous visit to the house of Cornelius and the opening up of the gospel to the Gentiles (Acts 10).

In Acts 12, Peter's old fishing partner, James, dies by the sword on the orders of King Herod of Judea. (He was a nephew of Herod Antipas, the ruler of Galilee who ordered the beheading of John the Baptist and became friends with Pilate during the trial of Jesus.) After the death of James, Peter was next in Herod's sights, but the Lord sent an angel to deliver him from prison. His time would come as Jesus had prophesied, but not yet.

Chapter 15 records Peter's last appearance in the book of Acts, when he participated in the Council at Jerusalem. The Jerusalem-based apostles and elders, along with Paul and Barnabas, had met to discuss the important question of whether new Gentile converts should be circumcised and required to keep the Law of Moses. By now, the other James (the Lord's brother) had become the clear leader of the Jerusalem church, but we find Peter making a pivotal contribution to the conference – one which reflected his journey.

After much discussion, Peter got up and addressed them: 'Brothers, you know that some time ago God made a choice among you that the Gentiles should hear from my lips the message of the gospel and believe. God, who knows the heart, showed that he accepted them by giving the Holy Spirit to them, just as he did to us. He did not discriminate between us and them, for he purified their hearts by faith. Now then, why do you try to test God by putting on the necks of Gentiles a yoke that neither we nor our ancestors have been able to bear? No! We believe it is through the grace of our Lord Jesus that we are saved, just as they are.'

(Acts 15:7–11)

Peter learned from Jesus the sweet sound of grace through unforgettable, personal experience and by revelation from the Holy Spirit. He will carry it in his heart for ever.

The keys of the kingdom were in hands that Jesus had been very careful to prepare.

Spoons, loons and elephants

Scattered around my study are reminders of countries I have visited in one form of ministry or another. There are colourful spoons from Poland; a ceramic loon from Canada; a pair of elephants from India (artefacts, you understand – my study isn't big enough for … never mind). Decorative chopsticks evoke memories of Japan. My boyhood days with missionary parents are also represented: a picture of the *Aquitania* departing Pier 54 in New York hangs behind my desk. We sailed on her from Southampton to Nova Scotia in 1949, en route for what was then the British West Indies. A map of Anguilla hangs on another wall.

But the object I value most sits in a little red box on a set of drawers. It is a lapel badge inscribed 'The Queen's Award for Voluntary Service', the MBE for volunteer groups. The strange thing is – I did absolutely nothing on the remarkable project in Wellingborough, Northants, for which the award was made in 2012. It happened like this.

My friend, Simon Trundle, owns and runs a successful business, leads a church and is founder and Chief Executive of the Hope Project.

Simon and his wife Bernie are devoted followers of Jesus; they live and breathe for his kingdom to come. Simon and Bernie had a vision for the transformation of an estate of 1,000 homes in the nearby town. It was a deeply deprived area, with many empty houses because no one wanted to live there. Through Simon's leadership and the sacrificial service of himself, his family, and the relatively small church committed to the area, the estate has been transformed to an amazing degree. Since 1997 youth crime rates have fallen by 50 per cent; there is no longer a gang terrorising people; drug dealing has been significantly reduced; amenities are much improved and many families are living new lives. Now there are 200 applications for every house that becomes available. And a good number of people have given their lives to Jesus. Hope has come and it was these achievements that were recognised and honoured by The Queen's Award for Voluntary Service, citing 'outstanding voluntary work in the community'.

I have known Simon for twenty years and during that period have had the privilege of discipling him, from the early days through to the present time. We have laughed and cried together and shared many meals together with his family in their home. I have watched the children grow up to become fine adults, all committed to the kingdom of God and serving Jesus in various spheres. His leadership of the church and the Hope Project has evolved and blossomed.

In a beautifully appointed skills centre on the estate (transformed from an old run-down community centre), the Vice Lord Lieutenant of Northamptonshire presented the award – an engraved crystal, along with a personal letter signed by Her Majesty, the Queen. Afterwards, Simon came to me and quietly placed in my hand the lapel badge. He had been entrusted with a small number of badges to give at his discretion to those who had given significant service in the Project. With characteristic generosity he considered that the existence of the project was due in some measure to my input into his life. The badge was a token of his gratitude. For those who worked so hard and gave so much of themselves to the people of the estate, the recognition granted by the Queen is highly valued and deservedly so. For me, Simon's gracious appreciation of having been discipled is beyond price.

Back to my study. Another picture, specially commissioned and given to me by the leaders of another Midlands church, hangs on the wall facing my desk. It is in the form of an artistic collage of shapes, including, among other things, a butterfly, European postage stamps, a Scripture reference significant to our relationship, and the single word, 'Grace'. It reminds me daily that it is only the grace of God, breathing through our relationships and our service, that achieves what is lasting in his glorious kingdom.

Go and disciple the nations

We began with the words of Jesus, commissioning his disciples shortly before he ascended to heaven.

> *All authority in heaven and on earth has been given to me.*
> *Therefore go and make disciples of all nations*
>
> **(Matt. 28:18–19)**

We have seen the example of Jesus discipling the Twelve – the model they had experienced and now understood. They knew what they had been called to do. We have observed how Jesus' discipleship of Peter was personal and authentic. It was challenging but it was hugely encouraging. It didn't happen haphazardly – it was intentional. It was strategic. And it changed his life.

To some the Lord may be saying even now – are you up for this? Do you want to be discipled at this level? To others he will be saying – who are you discipling? In whom are you investing what God has done in you? Are you being strategic? Jesus was – he chose carefully whom he would disciple, after a night of prayer. To others still, the challenge may be about being involved in both aspects – receiving and giving.

We have been sitting in on a Masterclass. Now we in the twenty-first century must ask ourselves – how does this affect our own lives, our churches and our generation?

....

The anointed servant – *reflections*

Being discipled

- The key that unlocked Peter's destiny was the anointing of the Holy Spirit. Whatever we have experienced of the Spirit so far, there is always more. Why not take time now to ask God for a fresh anointing, or find someone to pray with you?

- How does Peter's success and fulfilment make you feel – inspired or inadequate? If it is the latter, remember, you and I are not called to be Peter – we are called to be ourselves, our unique selves in Christ, enabled by the Spirit.

- As we come to the end of Jesus' Masterclass, what is God saying to you?

- What do you think is the next step for you?

Discipling others

- If you have seen those you have discipled being released into their future, you know the joy and fulfilment it brings. How could you develop this aspect of your life?

- Think about the question of being strategic. What adjustments or changes could you make that might make you more effective?

Chapter Seven
Can we follow Jesus' model today?

Discipleship in the twenty-first century

The practice of discipleship which emerges from observing Jesus' interaction with his chosen band may give rise to some understandable questions in our place and time. We will consider three.

'Wasn't the discipling of the Twelve a special case and not representative of what was to follow?'

It is certainly true that the Twelve had the special benefit of being discipled directly by Jesus and also carried the responsibility of leading the newly formed church after his return to heaven. But if we are motivated to see every single believer in Jesus being equipped to reach their full potential in personhood and ministry, surely the same principles apply. As we have already noted, Jesus' words in the Great Commission, operative to the end of the age, emphasise formation and training, ie process, rather than initiation only. If we are to see this age reach its climax with Jesus returning in his kingdom glory, I believe the same importance attaches to Jesus' example today as it did in the first century.

'Discipleship in this fashion must be time-intensive. Can we afford to make such a commitment in our modern, fast-paced world?'

In the light of Jesus' own strategy and its remarkable outcome, the answer must surely be, 'Can we afford not to?' As we have seen, the fruit of Jesus' patient training of the Twelve was the stability and inspired leadership of the first apostles in Jerusalem and beyond. Their presence and ministry undergirded the establishing of the Jerusalem church and the rapid increase in the number of disciples. Jesus' model demonstrates that investment in discipleship leads to exponential growth. If a packed programme is controlling our priorities, perhaps we need to stop and reflect and maybe take the longer view.

'Is discipleship of this kind possible in our church?'

For some, this may be the most practical and challenging question of all, given the diversity of tradition and structure across our church communities today. So how can we approach the challenge of radical discipleship in widely differing settings?

Varying structures can be more helpful or less helpful, but ultimately, I don't think structure is the issue. At the heart of discipleship is the nature of the kingdom of God. The practice of discipleship, Jesus-style, is more about the values and ethos which permeate and characterise a church. So let's ask ourselves instead, 'Is it possible to identify a *kingdom culture* in which discipleship can grow and flourish?' Values inform choices; choices lead to behaviour; behaviour creates culture. So what values, espoused in any setting, facilitate personal discipleship and indeed persuade us in that direction? As we discover more of the freedom which the Spirit brings, can we take measured but bold steps towards following Jesus' example? I believe we can.

Discipleship and community

Discipleship belongs in the church community. Whilst teaching has an important part to play and programmes of one kind or another can be helpful, there is nothing as effective as inter-personal relationships. And those relationships can be found within the security of the body of Christ.

In our churches we have Christians from different generations, men and women from all walks of life, some of whom have walked with God for many years; followers of Jesus with different levels of experience and maturity and with a variety of gifts and calling. The body represents a vast resource when it is released to its full potential, which makes radical discipleship possible. Leadership teams can lead the way by example and by helping to encourage and support appropriate and meaningful relationships across the community of disciples.

So far, we have explored Jesus' example in discipling the Twelve and his commissioning of the apostles to go and disciple the nations. We may be persuaded of its relevance and wish to develop it further, or introduce it, in our own church situation. Before we do so, however, we should remember that discipleship is only one element to consider when we talk about the nature of the kingdom of God. It is part of the rounded whole of kingdom life and attempts to press forward without considering other key aspects could be premature.

In Part Two we will seek to identify the nature of what we are calling a 'kingdom culture', and the kind of values which, though expressed in different traditions, will enable us to create and grow discipling communities. What are some of the elements that will characterise such a community and which require equal attention, if strategic discipleship is to be successful in the Church's life and mission?

We owe it to a new generation of followers of Jesus, hungry for radical Christianity, to look again at the implications of the Great Commission.

....

Can we follow Jesus' model today? – *reflections*

For leaders

- What do you believe is the relevance of Jesus' Masterclass to us today?

- Accepting the value of many external discipleship programmes, do you agree or disagree that discipleship primarily belongs in the church community?

- What might be the implications of seeking to implement such a model?

PART TWO
A DISCIPLING COMMUNITY

Can we follow Jesus' model today?

Is there a 'kingdom culture' in which discipleship will flourish?

What values, though expressed in diverse traditions, enable us to create and grow discipling communities?

Chapter Eight
A culture of grace and blessing

A charming sound

Whenever I hear the word 'discipleship' I want to hear the word 'grace' no more than a breath away. Everything begins and ends with grace – grace that flows like a river through our lives and carries us, into the ages to come (see Eph. 2:7).

The disciples had grown up in a culture which was shaped and dominated by temple, synagogue, tradition and religious leaders, who in turn classified everyone else in terms of their relationship to it. It was a culture which created an unforgiving, legalistic atmosphere, where there were endless rules to be observed and severe attitudes towards all who were deemed to have fallen short. Noncompliance placed a person beyond the pale and incurred from the Pharisees the demeaning label, 'sinners' – outcasts, a class of below-the-mark people, sometimes linked with the equally despised tax collectors, and definitely off the guest list.

But after the Master's call, for three years the disciples found themselves living in the pool of grace that surrounded Jesus – a different world from the one they had known growing up. The impact must have been overwhelming. Over and over again as they followed Jesus, they witnessed compassion, the tender touch, forgiveness, new freedoms and, above all, inclusion. And in their personal relationship with Jesus they experienced his constant care and love.

Doubtless, being discipled by Jesus involved them in all sorts of challenges, as issues of character and attitude were faced. Obedience was sometimes costly, as when they first left behind their normal occupations. Familiar points of security were being questioned, one after another; sacrifices were made. But their hearts had been captivated by grace and that changed everything. Along with the times of testing there were moments of incredible joy and blessing and wonder. How could they resist the invitation to be taught and shaped by the Master?

Discipleship flourishes in an atmosphere of grace; it withers in an environment of rules and regulations. When grace permeates a church community and the favour of God is resting there, it is a joy to respond to the opportunity of being discipled. Philip Doddridge, an early eighteenth-century Congregational minister and hymn writer, caught something when he wrote, rather quaintly: *'Grace! 'tis a charming sound, harmonious to the ear.'*

Radical discipleship and astonishing grace are inseparable in the kingdom of God. When we have experienced the 'charm' of God's grace, the whiff of condemnation or legalism is a foreign climate. When our own hearts are daily touched by the grace of Jesus towards us it will affect our relationships with our brothers and sisters. When leaders lead from hearts melted by grace, the beauty of grace fills the air. The letter that kills cannot coexist with the Spirit who gives life (2 Cor. 3:6). Where grace reigns, there is no place for the judgmental attitude or the pointing finger. In a culture of grace, the misuse of spiritual authority chimes strangely, like a cracked bell.

A personal story

After many years as a Christian, including preaching and teaching, I encountered the Holy Spirit and a revelation of grace in a new way that changed my life. I have sometimes described the first thirty years of my life as the making of a Pharisee; the last forty years, as a journey towards the Father's heart – a journey that is still going on.

When my father was two, his father was sent to the trenches in France and was dead within four weeks. That's the way it was in 1915

– the First World War was exacting its toll in blood. My grandmother did her best to bring up a two-year-old on her own and in the conditions she faced. The outcome was that my father grew up to become a headstrong, forceful character. When that was translated into his own family life, my brother and I found him authoritarian and dominating. As to physical discipline, he never touched us once – he didn't need to; his word was law from the cradle.

I spent most of my early life trying to reach standards, to meet expectations. I cannot remember moments of intimacy. To the best of my ability I conformed, but in the process I was crushed on the inside. Approaching adulthood, I had pretty much sunk without trace and, not surprisingly, my instinctive model of God was someone who required a lot and was not easy to satisfy.

Adding to the pressure were the expectations of a fairly rigid, evangelical church, which was strong on its particular form of ecclesiology, while exhorting us to maintain 'separation from the world'. My father, who had been converted to Christ at the age of thirty, became a missionary. Passionate, but a maverick still, he took us to the West Indies when I was nine years old. From the age of twelve I was preaching and studying Scripture; by my mid-twenties, back in the UK, I had a growing teaching ministry. Looking back, the level of certainty about everything I believed was frightening. But the truth is, underneath it all I was the original screwed up missionary kid; my public ministry was outstripping by some way my actual experience of God.

When I was twenty-nine years old my father died. I had been married for eight years, with little of the early damage repaired. It was after turning thirty that God graciously met with me. I had been the speaker for a summer week in a hotel in Devon, where for five nights I spoke on eschatology, beginning with 'the rapture'. It was all gripping stuff and the large lounge was packed every night. On the Thursday evening a man of God came through and after patiently listening to me delivering another large chunk of exciting images and apocalyptic scenarios, he sought me out. With remarkable grace, he gently placed an arm across my shoulders and said, 'Do you know – I used to believe all that once and I had to throw it all overboard.' He didn't say much more, except to leave me with a blessing and a smile.

Upstairs in my room I fell on my knees, not knowing what had hit me. God had got through the armour. Back at home in Bristol that weekend, my wife and I attended the last night of what we used to call a 'gospel campaign', conducted by Hugh Thompson, a prophetic church leader in the city. At the appeal I was first out, on my knees at the front. Hugh, who knew me just well enough to know I was in ministry (and later became a good friend), asked me why I was there. I told him I didn't know – I was just seeking God. Very simply he placed his hands on my head and prayed that I might be filled with the Holy Spirit and that the Lord would set me free from the *'ism'* of the past. He named it, but it could have been any. (So often in the life of a church, there are the good things and then the *'ism'* bit.)

As Hugh prayed, the Lord poured out his Spirit and something like fire went through the centre of my being. I can't begin to tell you what it meant to me. In the 1904 Welsh revival they sang the hymn, *Here is love, vast as the ocean*. It includes the lines, 'Grace and love like mighty rivers, poured incessant from above'. It felt like that. I just couldn't get over his love and, forty years later, I still can't.

Soon after, I got to know people like the late Arthur Wallis, John Noble, Gerald Coates and others like them, leading figures in the early house church movement in the UK. There was a fresh sound emerging, about committed relationships, openness and vulnerability in the body of Christ, in which family came before ministry; loving relationships which were more important than ticking off points of doctrine. There were new insights into the nature of Church. The kingdom of God was future and yet coming now! The good news of the kingdom was about transforming individuals *and* society. Above all there was a fresh revelation of grace which, for me, was overwhelming.

I began to discover what my heavenly Father was really like.

Songs were being written to express what the Holy Spirit was saying and doing. I remember singing through the tears:

Grace it seems, is all he has, and one big open heart;
and it's so good being loved by you my Lord

We are moving on into a new appreciation
of the love that flows from Father out to every child of God.[1]

I love him more now, after I've sinned,
for I've found out what he is really like;
He's disposed to forgive all the sins of my life,
and I can put my full trust in him now.[2]

Muriel found a difference. Prior to that, she had suffered because I put my ministry before her and our family: now all that began to change. Our three children lost a disciplinarian and gained a father. As the grace of God changed me, it began to change my ministry; the arrogance began to melt. I was sharing from the heart, but also sharing the journey of those to whom I had the privilege of ministering. I was learning by experience that the Christian life is not lived by observing rules, but from an inward response to God's grace, inspired by the Holy Spirit; that our living and serving is not to earn the blessing of God (consciously or subconsciously) but to express the devotion of hearts captivated by love.

And it was in the embrace of my heavenly Father that I began to discover who I really was. For the first time I knew what it was to be truly at peace with myself – still a work in progress, but at peace. To fear that the teaching of grace might lead to the spread of licence is never to have understood true grace.

As the relationship between Muriel and me and John and Christine developed, and the opportunity arose to be helped and discipled by them, we were only too glad to respond. In a climate of grace we can talk through real issues with mutual trust and without pressure.

There is truth and reality, but also love, honour and encouragement. When grace is flowing, the response to discipleship is not one of fear or apprehension, but the delight of a willing heart. For me, the healing process was continuing. I remember the day when I looked outward and upward and said, 'I forgive you, Dad'. The memories of the past were healed and now I am looking forward to meeting him again. We have some things to talk about and I guess, by now, he has too. And we will worship Jesus side by side.

Discipleship is not about learning a list of dos and don'ts, ticking the boxes and feeling good about it, or missing out on a few boxes and feeling guilty. That is legal country. Discipleship is moving forward a step at a time, discovering the heart of Jesus, learning to enjoy the presence of God, being helped to live from the Spirit within; and being taught from Scripture what pleases the Lord. We begin to find God's law written on our hearts and gradually flowing down the slope of personality: making mistakes, getting it wrong sometimes, but with our hand in his and surrounded by the body of Christ.

Grace is at the heart of kingdom culture and in such a culture, discipleship can thrive.

....

A culture of grace and blessing – *reflections*

For the church community

- On a personal level, it may be that my own story has touched issues that you have faced in the past and which continue to affect your life today. Could this be your moment to open your heart to a fresh experience of the Father's love and grace and allow him to bring a deeper release?

- The grace message is about living life under the blue sky of the Father's smile, without a breath of condemnation.

Take a moment to reflect on his love and forgiveness. It would be good to pray with someone.

For leaders

- How has your personal experience of grace shaped your ministry?

- Does the church community you lead reflect the freedoms and fellowship of grace? Would a visitor describe the church as static or journeying?

- If you are concerned that the church may be hampered by some unhelpful aspects of tradition (ancient or modern!), or by legalistic attitudes, has God given you faith to see the Holy Spirit opening a way through to new things?

- What steps could you take to lead the way?

[1] Extract taken from the song *We Are Moving On* by Ian Traynar, copyright © 1985 Thankyou Music.

[2] Extract taken from the song *Why Should I Lose My First Love* by Ian Traynor, copyright © 1977 Thankyou Music.

Chapter Nine

A culture shaped by the good news of the kingdom

The call to discipleship

At first glance, the Jesus of the Gospels is a paradox. On the one hand, grace simply flowed from him, in word and deed. Against all the prevailing norms in society, he reached out to the untouchables of his day with kindness and compassion. He was inclusive in ways that challenge us all. He spoke words of forgiveness to people who could otherwise only dream of receiving it; he offered generous love unexpectedly, whether feeding the hungry at the end of a long day, or healing the leper shunned by everyone else. He was close to the poor and was loved by the needy; in the words of the psalmist, his lips were 'anointed with grace' (Psa. 45:2).

Yet at the same time, his call to discipleship was presented in astonishingly clear terms, which left no one in any doubt about what Jesus was looking for in those who were making up their minds about following him. He made demands of people. He expected from those who wanted to be his disciples a level of radical commitment, which was always going to be costly. In his classic book *The Cost of Discipleship*, Dietrich Bonhoeffer said, 'When Christ calls a man he bids him come and die'.[1]

Listen to Jesus' invitation:

> *Large crowds were travelling with Jesus, and turning to them*
> *he said: 'If anyone comes to me and does not hate father and*
> *mother, wife and children, brothers and sisters – yes, even*

their own life – such a person cannot be my disciple. And whoever does not carry their cross and follow me cannot be my disciple. Suppose one of you wants to build a tower. Won't you first sit down and estimate the cost ... those of you who do not give up everything you have cannot be my disciples.'

(Luke 14:25–28,33)

The call of Jesus was absolute – it involved putting him before every relationship and every personal interest; wiggle room was zero. His words admitted no compromise, they couldn't be misunderstood. He didn't say, 'It would be helpful *if* , but, 'He cannot *be* my disciple unless'. Unqualified commitment was the only way to follow him. We have an example of Jesus following through on what he said, in the case of a particular enquirer. Luke tells us he was a ruler, evidently successful at an early age. The young man was genuine and asked the kind of question evangelists pray every morning to be asked that day.

As Jesus started on his way, a man ran up to him and fell on his knees before him. 'Good teacher,' he asked, 'what must I do to inherit eternal life?'

(Mark 10:17)

They talked about the commandments and then Mark says (10:21–22):

Jesus looked at him and loved him. 'One thing you lack,' he said. 'Go, sell everything you have and give to the poor, and you will have treasure in heaven. Then come, follow me.' At this the man's face fell. He went away sad, because he had great wealth.

Something about this young man drew out the love of Jesus in a way which observers noticed and remembered. But Jesus had discerned an area of his life that was going to be difficult for the prosperous, rising star and brought it into the light. The young man stood there, a struggle going on in his heart at the thought of giving away his unusually substantial possessions. Finally he walked away, unwilling to surrender everything; the price of following Jesus was too high. The most telling thing in the story is that Jesus watched him go, containing love's disappointment, not calling him back to renegotiate the terms of discipleship. We don't know if they ever met again.

In vivid contrast, after meeting Jesus, an eminent Pharisee from Tarsus was immediately baptised, 'calling on his name'. The same man, now called Paul, said later, 'whatever were gains to me I now consider loss for the sake of Christ' (Acts 22:16; Phil. 3:7). He started right and finished well, too.

How would I respond to that young seeker in similar circumstances today? Would I try to lead him into a confession of faith, thinking that we could come back to the issue of submitting his finances to Jesus at some point in the future?

The word of the kingdom

It is a poignant story which leaves us facing a question. What message are we proclaiming at the threshold? Because, in time, the message will shape the community. A call to true discipleship farther down the line may come as a shock to the system if the good news has been communicated as something less than the clear challenge of repentance and all-out commitment to Christ. In the parable of the sower, Jesus spoke about the farmer scattering the seed. The point of the parable has to do with the different kinds of soil on which the seed fell, but when Jesus interprets it he begins by describing the seed itself as 'the word of the kingdom' (Matt. 13:19, NASB). The kingdom is the reign of God. The good news begins with a very personal challenge: who is going to run my life in future?

The book of Acts begins with Peter announcing to everyone in Jerusalem that 'God had made this Jesus', *Lord* (Acts 2:36). Then he proceeded to call for the most radical turnaround imaginable, since they were the ones who had crucified him. The book ends with Paul spending two years at the hub of the Roman Empire, boldly preaching the kingdom of *God* (Acts 28:30–31). The good news of Jesus is actually about a change of government on earth; it's a message which challenges an empire, a nation, or a single life.

The 'word of the kingdom' touches us all. I recall moments when Muriel and I, like many other Christians, faced decisions that carried a price tag, but were significant to the rest of our lives. Such an occasion was a choice we faced in our early thirties, after I had received a fresh experience of the Spirit when Hugh Thompson prayed for me. We realised that God had brought him into our lives at that time and that there was much we needed to learn. We were living in a pleasant spot in Downend, Bristol, on the east side of the city. Hugh and Rosemary lived at Patchway on the northern edge of Bristol, where they were church planting. Their generously open home was in the middle of a council estate that was a very different environment from the one we were accustomed to.

I shared with Muriel one day that I felt God was calling us to sell up and move, to be part of the new church plant and, specifically, to be alongside Hugh and Rosemary. There would be implications for our family – Stephen was eight, Andrew, five, and Sarah, two. We prayed about it together over a period of time. Eventually, Muriel said that she hadn't received specific confirmation from God, but if I believed I had heard God she would support me in a move. It was incredibly loyal and brave on her part. With my heart in my mouth I said we would go. Soon, we were living in a house about two or three hundred yards from Hugh and Rosemary and became part of the small house church. Stephen was transferred to the local school and Andrew began there.

Concrete walls on the estate were disfigured by unsavoury graffiti. There were elements in the community whose behaviour was poor. It wasn't long before Andrew was coming home from school with bruises.

It was a tough time. Walking along the main road through the estate one day, with Sarah in her pushchair, Muriel cried inwardly to God. She said, 'God, if you don't speak to me I can't do this'. And God spoke to her. He said that our children were safer in the centre of his will than in the best residential area in Bristol. From that moment she had perfect peace and we faced each new day with the confidence that God was watching over us.

The move proved to be a key turning point in our lives. We learned so much about what God was saying and doing and our lives changed course. We got to know a number of prophetic leaders who would be significant to our growth and development. One of them was John Noble, the man who would become my spiritual father and a lasting influence on my life. Our three children are now grown up, married and, with their spouses, sold out to the values of the kingdom and to serving the Lord. Along the way, they have presented us with eight fantastic grandchildren. God has been gracious and we are grateful he led us the way he did.

When we yield to Jesus as Lord, we place our lives in his hands and discover that his love is faithful.

Where he reigns

We see it first in Old Testament prophecy:

> *How beautiful on the mountains are the feet of those who*
> *bring good news, who proclaim peace, who bring good tidings,*
> *who proclaim salvation, who say to Zion, 'Your God reigns!'*
>
> **(Isa. 52:7)**

The good news for Jerusalem was that *God* reigns and under his rule his people will find peace and salvation.

The message to the nations was the same: 'Why do the nations conspire and the peoples plot in vain? ... I have installed my king ... Serve the LORD ... Kiss his son ... Blessed are all who take refuge in him'

(Psa. 2:1,6,11–12). By kneeling before the King and becoming obedient to him, the nations would find refuge and blessing under his rule.

When God's chosen king arrived in person, he proclaimed the good news that the active reign of God was now here on earth. It showed itself first in an explosion of generosity, because God is like that.

> *Jesus went throughout Galilee, teaching in their synagogues, proclaiming the good news of the kingdom, and healing every disease and illness among the people. News about him spread all over Syria, and people brought to him all who were ill with various diseases, those suffering severe pain, the demon-possessed, those having seizures, and the paralysed; and he healed them.*
>
> **(Matt. 4:23–24)**

The first evidence of God's rule breaking in through the life of Jesus was the blessing that cascaded outwards, everywhere he went, enveloping people in waves of healing and release and great joy! Salvation flows when Jesus is acting in the authority God gave him. There are good news stories everywhere. Isaac Watts' inspired imagination soared with the idea:

> *Blessings abound where'er He reigns;*
> *The prisoner leaps to loose his chains;*
> *The weary find eternal rest;*
> *And all the sons of want are blest.*[2]

This kingdom, this reign of blessing, is the treasure which a man discovered in the field, and for which, out of sheer joy, he sells everything he has. It's the pearl of great value for which the merchant is prepared to lose all else.

So the message of Jesus is about finding salvation when we hand over the reins of our lives to him. It is about being governed by someone else and discovering under his rule freedom and wholeness through the work of his Spirit within. The salvation story is good news because the reign of God is transforming. The Jesus of the Gospels calls for total commitment from those who would follow him, and freely offers unconditional love, forgiveness and healing. Grace holds the door open wide for us to bow the knee to the King of Love. Surrendering to him is for our eternal good.

But the good news goes on! When we become his we receive the gift of the Holy Spirit, who *enables* us day by day to fulfil the desires of the King, to live in his kingdom with peace and joy. The Spirit sets us free from the downward spiral of sin and death and gives us wings to fly (see Rom. 8:1–2).

The seed – 'the word of the kingdom' – contains much more; it is about social justice and righteousness; about the transformation of society and a new order – God's order. But at its heart it is the simple announcement that love has triumphed over evil and now – God reigns!

Following in the footsteps of the King

The remarkable thing about Jesus' example is the way he combined his ministry of love and grace with the clarity of his message about justice, right living and radical discipleship. The tone changed sometimes, when he was confronting hypocrisy or greed, but those who felt their desperate need of him always felt welcome in his presence, never intimidated. His serving heart was as attractive as his message was challenging. He spoke with love and compassion, but the cost of following was there, too. The word of the kingdom was complete.

The challenge for us is to find the same wholeness in our lifestyle and message. We seek to model his love in acts of service and generosity in the communities around us, while at the same time, declaring the good news of Jesus, who is Saviour and Lord.

Phrases like 'belonging before believing' and 'journey' are all helpful and challenge us to be like Jesus in his inclusive grace. They are words we need to hear. But in our response, let's not lose the clarity of the kingdom message which he also proclaimed. It cost Jesus everything to be able to offer us forgiveness and salvation. It will cost us everything to follow him, as Bonhoeffer discovered, more than most, when he was executed on 9 April 1945.

It was the year I gave my young life to Christ.

Discipleship will flourish in a church community which has been shaped by the good news of the kingdom. It will be a different challenge if a lesser gospel has been preached. Jesus spoke of forgiveness and a change of lifestyle: 'neither do I condemn you … Go now and leave your life of sin' (John 8:11). He described the true measure of love: 'If you love me, keep my commands' (John 14:15).

For some, the first step toward developing discipleship in the Jesus *model* might be to revisit the Jesus *message*. Discipleship flourishes in a culture shaped by the good news of the kingdom of God.

....

A culture shaped by the good news of the kingdom
– reflections

For the church community

- The call to surrender everything to Jesus challenges us all – in different ways at different stages of life. Is the Lord speaking to you about a specific issue (perhaps something you have been aware of for a while)? Talk to him about it, or, if it would help, share it with others, or with one other person who can stand with you.

- Fresh acts of obedience delight the heart of Jesus. He wants you to know he appreciates those heart responses to him made in the secret place, especially when they have been costly. Do you have a personal story that would bless and encourage others?

For leaders

- What influences have shaped the church you lead, historically or recently? Are they contributing to the advance of God's kingdom?

- What do you think about Jesus' response to the young ruler? How would you see the implications for the twenty-first century?

- To what extent does the preaching and teaching in your church, or witness beyond its walls, reflect the clarity of Jesus' kingdom message?

- How does your church combine serving the needs of the community with proclaiming the good news of Jesus? Are the two activities identified with each other? How do they connect?

- If your church is already excited about living out the good news of the kingdom, how can the enthusiasm be channelled into significant discipleship paths?

[1] Dietrich Bonhoeffer, *The Cost of Discipleship* (Translation SCM Press, 2001) p44.

[2] Isaac Watts, *Jesus shall reign where'er the sun*, *Redemption Hymnal* (Assemblies of God Publishing House, Revised Edition 1955, Reprinted 1958).

Chapter Ten
A culture of faithful relationships

Starter for ten

You can never find a collective noun for theologians when you need one. What could it be?

A *school* (one for the dolphin lovers)? Sounds promising …

A *convocation* (as in eagles)? A bit high-flying, perhaps …

A *cloud* (bats)? Theologians *can* cloud the issue at times …

A *streak* (tigers)? That *really* doesn't work …

A *family* (beavers)? Well, sometimes, though not always, to be honest …

A group of theologians, by any other name, were brought together, tasked with coming up with one word which sums up the gospel. Their discussions would have ranged over different aspects of the salvation story, but the word they settled on was 'relationships'. And that was pure inspiration.

Last Sunday morning I was sitting in an aisle seat in church, the worship due to begin in two or three minutes. My friend, Malcolm, came by, ruffled my hair, said, 'Hi, curly – nice jacket' and carried on to his seat without stopping. Soon after, we were both engaged in worshipping the Lord. Apart from being clear evidence of his sartorial taste (and discounting the fact that I keep my hair too short to be remotely curly), the gesture was an expression of true friendship, as real as the worship that followed. Church and genuine relationships belong together – the one is an expression of the other.

Made in his image

If there is an ultimate definition of God, it is found in the simple but sublime words of 1 John 4:8: 'God is love'. Emil Brunner, a Swiss theologian, described those three words as, 'the most daring statement that has ever been made in human language'.[1] Those three amazing words take us into the very essence – the inner life – of the triune God and their relationship with each other. The Father loves the Son, the Spirit loves the Father, the Son loves the Spirit; they love each other intimately and faithfully. God *is* love. It was so before creation; it has always been so, without beginning.

In his classic work on the Holy Spirit, *Flame of Love*, Clark Pinnock says, 'We begin with the identity of the Spirit as a divine Person in a social Trinity ... What loveliness and sheer liveliness God is! ... Each person of the Trinity exists eternally with the others, each has its gaze fixed on the others, each casts a glance away from itself in love to the others, the eye of each lover ever fixed on the beloved other.'[2]

Above everything else, God is relational. His nature is to share life. 'Early theologians spoke of the divine nature as a dance, a circling round of threefold life, as a coming and going among the persons.'[3] Creation was about God's love expanding into a new sphere – a physical sphere, the cosmos and the world we live in; embracing a man and a woman and the race which would issue from them, drawing us into the divine dance. The 'big bang' that matters was the explosion of divine love, out of eternity into time; out of the unseen realm into the visible. The life of the triune God would for ever overflow in giving and receiving. We would be free to respond to his loving advances and to enter into an enriching and fulfilling relationship with him, and he with us. That was the heart of God.

But by definition, we would also be free to choose another path, because, in any relationship, true love and total control are wholly incompatible – they exclude each other. The tragedy of the human story is that, seduced by the lure of independence, we used that God-given freedom, not to love him, but to walk away; and a God whose love had made him utterly vulnerable, because love is like that, wept. But the story didn't end there. Faithful still, God stood ready at the cross to pay the price of love, to bring the lost ones home to the Father's house.

To God, relationships are everything. When we talk about the importance of relationships in the Church, we are not considering one of the style choices for doing church – we are at the foundation of who God is. Those theologians really were inspired – the gospel is an invitation to share in a new community of love. At the heart of that community, through the Holy Spirit, is our relationship with the Father and with his Son, and by the same Spirit we are also joined to one another. We express the life of God. Made in God's image, made for shared life, made to love and be loved, made to be truly fulfilled through relationship with others. That is why relationships in the body of Christ are more important than our ecclesiological preferences; they are more important than what we personally achieve. Our relationships are intended to reflect in the created world the nature of the triune God.

And that is why a culture of loving relationships delights the Father's heart, provides a healthy environment in which we can grow, and powerfully nurtures discipleship.

The fledgling church

Luke describes what life was like following the explosive, early growth of the Church.

> *Everyone was filled with awe ... All the believers were together and had everything in common. They sold property and possessions to give to anyone who had need. Every day they continued to meet together in the temple courts. They broke bread in their homes and ate together with glad and sincere hearts, praising God and enjoying the favour of all the people.*
>
> **(Acts 2:43–47)**

All the believers were one in heart and mind ... With great
power the apostles continued to testify to the resurrection of
the Lord Jesus.

(Acts 4:32–33)

The early disciples were evidently sharing a great deal of their lives; generous and caring, one in mind and heart, opening their homes, enjoying friendship around the meal table, praying and worshipping together. The lifestyle of the community of believers was a striking platform from which the apostles could proclaim the good news. And the people liked what they saw – it was that good.

In the early seventies, Muriel and I had become part of what was then a small house church of about thirty people, meeting in Hugh and Rosemary Thompson's home on the Patchway estate, on the northern edge of Bristol. We were reaching for something like the kind of relational community that Acts 2 describes – a community which is relationship oriented first, rather than meeting oriented first and last. We recognised the importance of gathered church and have always done so, but wanted to see those gatherings based on genuine relationship and real friendship, providing the basis for mission and growth.

Somehow, it wasn't happening the way we hoped. So it was decided that, as a once-off thing, we would suspend meetings for twelve weeks, encouraging everyone to spend the time, instead, finding one another as people, sharing some aspect of life together, getting to know more about what made each other tick. They might want to go to the supermarket together, or perhaps a concert; or go for a walk in the woods with another family, or pray or break bread together. After some initial consternation at the idea, there was a good response and we were able to give it a try. It was quite a remarkable experience. We actually reverted to having our normal meetings again after seven weeks or so, but something happened through that very practical lesson.

As a community we learned something about the true nature of our commitment to one another. We looked each other in the eye with a different awareness. The house church in Patchway went on to link with another such group not far away and in time became a substantial church in the city. A few years later, Stuart Lindsell wrote a helpful book called, *Relationships – Jesus Style*, which summed up what we were learning and has influenced my approach to Chapter Eleven.[4]

Our brief experiment in the early days isn't something I am recommending; it was simply a temporary measure which we felt was right at a particular moment in a particular situation. As a church grows larger, the challenge of personal relationships across a bigger community grows with it anyway, as the house church movement discovered, and will be met in different ways. But the truth remains that the reality of genuine relationships in the body of Christ will be at the heart of a church which seeks to truly reflect the love of God and the good news of Jesus.

Being discipled in such a community anchors the process of discipleship in real life alongside real people and helps us on our journey to wholeness.

Personal relationships

If your experience is like mine you will have twigged that working it all out in our personal lives doesn't run quite as smoothly as it appeared to do at the beginning of the book of Acts! (You have to say 'beginning' because they had their own issues later.) There used to be an old saying:

> *To dwell above with saints we love, O that will be glory;*
> *To dwell below with saints we know is quite another story.*

Ain't *that* the truth! Eschatology aside (the end of Revelation talks about God coming *down* to dwell with us in a renewed creation, not us going *up*!), the point rings true. The reality is, the closer we come to one another, stuff comes to the surface – our insecurities, our fears, our weaknesses, our sins (there – I've said it!). I remember Gerald Coates talking about personal relationships many years ago. He was describing three phases through which our relationships sometimes pass. First, *veneer*, when we are exchanging the social signals, being polite and courteous – all well intended and genuine but essentially on the surface at that stage. Second, *disillusion*, as we get to know each other better, discover more about each other and, at some point, feel let down. Then the choice: we can retreat to a manageable distance, as so often happens, or we can press through to a third phase. It's called *reality*.

I suggest there are seven elements which will be found in real life relationships and we will explore them in the next chapter. But before we do so, we need to notice one other aspect.

Corporate unity – one in heart and mind

The disciples in the Jerusalem church not only shared their lives, they were also of one mind – they shared a common understanding and vision. Recognising the importance of personal relationships has a huge bearing on our corporate unity. It will shape our attitudes and behaviour when we face the challenge of agreeing about issues that affect the whole church, such as a shared sense of direction, or uniting behind immediate goals. Sometimes, with the best will in the world, there will be genuine disagreement.

Being passionate about what we think the church's priorities should be, or what it should be doing in a given locality, is a good thing. It can also be dangerous if it is hijacked by the enemy to cause division. Often, differing concerns or passions are not either/or, but both/and, like, for example, Word and Spirit, social action and proclamation – *being* good news and *telling* good news, or 'works' and 'wonders'. (I still remember the feeling of helplessness some years ago, watching a young church I had been trying to help, as it foundered over just such an issue of differing priorities, knowing there was nothing I could do to prevent the breakup.) The truth is, such things belong together, and maintaining tender hearts helps us to embrace each other's emphases.

But in many practical areas there are real choices to be made as we listen to God and seek to know his will. We may all be passionate about investing resources in the advance of the kingdom, but between us we will have different priorities, all valid, regarding the most pressing needs, the most urgent challenges. When we are committed to holding through on our relationships, we will have an equal concern about *how* we hold our perspectives, *how* we communicate them and *how* we respect different views. You know you are in trouble when you suddenly realise that ensuring your views come out on top has become more important than anything else. That's when the kingdom loses out. That's when, as they say, we need to wake up and smell the coffee. As my friend, Hugh, once prayed, 'Deliver us, Lord, from the tyranny of our own point of view!'

A culture of faithful relationships supports the natural tensions of church planting and growth when, understandably, we are all looking at situations through the eyes of our own history and gifting. Enduring relationships are the foundation of everything we want to achieve. Time and attention given to nurturing them is the soundest investment of all, because everything else springs from our unity in the Spirit.

'One in heart' – let's begin there and live there. And from that place we will seek to hear the Lord, directly and through each other, and look to become *'one in mind'.* And so long as differences of understanding remain, we will continue by his grace to love and honour one another and walk humbly.

Faithful relationships are foundational to developing a discipling community.

....

A culture of faithful relationships *– reflections*

For the church community
- Reflecting on what has been said about being made in the image of God, do you agree, or disagree, with the practical

conclusions? What is your understanding of what it means to be made in God's image?

- What has been your experience of relationships in the context of church? What would you like to see emerge, that may not be happening at the moment?

- *Veneer, disillusion, reality* – how did you respond to the picture painted by those words? Thinking of your own current relationships in the church, are there ways in which you would like to move forward?

For leaders

- Our understanding of the nature of God will shape our understanding of the nature of Church. If your church was the very first to be visited by a stranger from another culture, what impression of God would they take away?

- How would you assess the relational unity of your church at this time? Is the quality of interpersonal relationships regarded as a significant part of oversight responsibility?

- Would you say that your church is essentially of one mind regarding the kind of church you aspire to be and the corporate vision for its mission? If there are areas of concern, what steps might you take to strengthen the foundation?

---

[1] Emil Brunner, *Dogmatics, vol. 1, The Christian Doctrine of God*, trans. Olive Wyon, (Philadelphia: Westminster Press, 1949).

[2] Clark H. Pinnock, *Flame of Love* (InterVarsity Press, 1996) pp22,42.

[3] Ibid. p22.

[4] Stuart Lindsell, *Relationships – Jesus Style* (Word (UK) Ltd/Pioneer, 1992).

Chapter Eleven
A culture of faithful relationships – seven elements

A number of practical strands go to make up enduring relationships, which, in turn, provide a secure environment for discipleship.

1. Commitment

'They devoted themselves to … fellowship' (Acts 2:42).

When we became Christians, our first experience of commitment was *ours to God*. We yielded our lives to Jesus and set out to follow him. As we went along, we became aware of another kind of commitment – *God's to us*. We heard him saying in the New Covenant, 'I will be their God' (Heb. 8:10). We learned of his amazing promise: 'Never will I leave you' (Heb. 13:5). Paul's words to Timothy just blew us away: 'if we are faithless, he remains faithful, for he cannot disown himself' (2 Tim. 2:13). Every day of our journey we experienced God's faithful love; his example redefines commitment.

Then we discovered a third area of commitment – *ours to one another.* As fellow disciples in community, our primary commitment is not to a doctrinal statement, nor to a vision, however inspiring, nor to a model of church, but to one another. God's kingdom and Satan's kingdom can be summed up in two words – fusion and fission. God is all about joining together, Satan is all about splitting apart.

'But he who is joined to the Lord becomes one spirit with him' (1 Cor. 6:17, ESV).

'For this reason a man will leave his father and mother and be joined to his wife, and the two will become one flesh' (Eph. 5:31, NRSV).

'In him the whole building is joined together and rises to become a holy temple in the Lord' (Eph. 2:21–22).

'All the believers were one' (Acts 4:32).

The early believers shared their lives together and were committed to one another on every level. When we gather as Church we don't leave our lives at the door, as though this is a retreat from life into a different dimension. Church is where shared life, in all its aspects, finds its expression. We bring our victories and challenges, our aspirations and weaknesses, our families, jobs (or pressure to find one), our histories, our hopes – everything, into the presence of God with his people; and we worship the Lord, hear from him by his Spirit and encourage one another. Mutual love in the Spirit is the cement that holds us together. Our commitment is to one another.

George Elliott's words express the beauty of real friendship: 'Oh the comfort, the inexpressible comfort, of feeling safe with a person; having neither to weigh thoughts nor measure words. But pour them out, just as they are, chaff and grain together, knowing that a faithful hand will take and sift them, keep what is worth keeping, and then with the breath of kindness, blow the rest away.'

In Chapter Three we saw how Jesus and Peter became friends. Peter was being discipled in the context of a relationship of love and trust, rather like the relationships which marked out the beginnings of the Jerusalem church. In such a culture, the shared experience of life and faith strengthens us in our individual growth as disciples of Jesus.

2. Acceptance

'Accept one another, then, just as Christ accepted you' (Rom. 15:7).

If we are going to be committed to one another as members of the body of Christ, it follows that we can only begin by accepting each other. Sometimes we have enormous differences, our backgrounds and life experience can be like chalk and cheese; but in Christ we are one family. Do you remember how Jesus accepted you when you came to him – weaknesses, mistakes, disappointments, sins and all? We were so different from him, but he just wrapped his arms around us and loved us and promised he would never leave us. Now he asks us to accept one another in the same way.

Some find it difficult to believe that such a level of acceptance could possibly include *them*. Many years ago I came across a simple diagram.

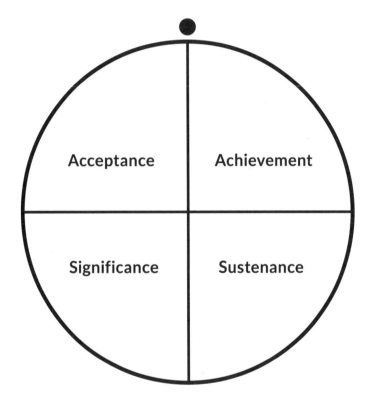

The enemy wants us to get into wrong thinking. Starting at the top and heading clockwise, it goes like this. If only I could *achieve* something really good, something that others will notice – that would keep me going, it would *sustain* me; at last I would have *significance* and then I would be *accepted*. The sad thing is that, going that way round, we will repeat the cycle for a whole lifetime. All the while, the Holy

Spirit is whispering; 'Wrong direction! Begin with acceptance and *go the other way*'. I am *accepted* in Jesus (and so by his family, too); it's a given, it's the foundation of our lives; *that* is what gives us *significance*, that is what *sustains* us; and with that assurance, enabled by his Spirit, the way is wide open for us to *achieve* all that he wants us to be.

I want to be part of a church where we can be ourselves, make our mistakes, forgive and be forgiven and press on together towards the goal. In the family of Jesus' disciples we accept one another because we have all received his grace. Discipleship will thrive in an atmosphere of loving acceptance.

3. Honour

'Honour one another above yourselves' (Rom. 12:10).

We honour one another by taking each other seriously, by giving each other our full attention, by listening to each other. Very often it is the small things that demonstrate mutual honour – the body language, the gesture, the unhurried response. Paul wanted the Ephesian Christians to 'Submit to one another out of reverence for Christ' (Eph. 5:21). When we look into the face of another brother or sister, we are looking at someone in whom the Creator dwells. Mutual honour is part of the discipling ethos.

4. Encouragement

'encourage one another and build each other up, just as in fact you are doing' (1 Thess. 5:11).

'But encourage one another daily' (Heb. 3:13).

So who have you encouraged today? We all need it, whether we are mature Christians who have been on the road for many years, or new Christians just starting out. When we encourage each other we reinforce each other's strengths; for a moment we add our shoulder to someone else's wheel and it turns a little faster. Paul tells us that encouragement is the nature of prophecy: 'the one who prophesies speaks to people for their strengthening, encouraging and comfort' (1 Cor. 14:3). When we encourage someone else we are in tune with the Spirit's voice. Encouragement is the stuff of discipleship.

5. Openness and transparency

'We continually ask God ... so that you may live a life worthy of the Lord and please him in every way ... giving joyful thanks to the Father, who has qualified you to share in the inheritance of his holy people in the kingdom of light' (Col. 1:9–12).

The kingdom of God is a kingdom of light and it produces a culture of openness and transparency. The wonderful thing is that because of the blood of Jesus we are forgiven and cleansed, and actually qualified to live in this kingdom! Paul sums it up: 'now you are light in the Lord. Live as children of light' (Eph. 5:8).

There is a level of openness we need to have with all of God's people and a deeper level with some, particularly those who are involved in our pastoral care or who may be discipling us.

'he ... showed me the Holy City, Jerusalem, coming down out of heaven from God. It shone with the glory of God ... the great street of the city was of gold, as pure as transparent glass' (Rev. 21:10–11,21).

Trying to convey the purity of the gold in the prophetic picture of God's people in the age to come, John describes it as being 'transparent glass'. We can, if we choose, go in and out of church for years and hide away from reality, but to walk on the streets of the city that God is building is to walk on transparent glass. It is the path of the true disciple – living a life of openness. So often, insecurities within can be masked by an outward strength.

When I was still in business, I found myself one day on yet another training course. One afternoon session was entitled, 'Behavioural Analysis'. The lady presenter built up a diagram in stages, illustrating a life, and the final picture, with its four areas, looked like this:

Known to me and to others	Known to me but not to others
Open	**Hidden**
Blind	**Dark**
Known to others but not to me	Unknown to me or to others

Then she looked at the group of managers, of varying levels of seniority, and said, 'The optimum is to live life in the open square'. By now my ears were tingling – this sounded remarkably like God's kingdom! The kingdom of light is about life in the 'Open' square!

So what is the way forward if there are areas of our lives which fit in the 'Hidden' square? The challenge is to talk to those who care for us; to share the things that we are finding difficult to overcome and invite what help we may need.

As for the 'Blind' spots – we all have them! That is why, in my own life, there are people I trust to whom I have given the right to offer any personal observation, or ask any question at any time, which I will answer as honestly as I can. I have worked out that if others see in me unhelpful things of which I am unaware, the sooner I know, the better!

The last square, which in the business seminar was labelled 'Dark', need not disturb us. We can trust our loving, heavenly Father. David prayed in Psalm 139:23–24: 'Search me, God, and know my heart; test me and know my anxious thoughts. See if there is any offensive way in me, and lead me in the way everlasting.' We are in safe hands. David was a lover of God; he had already said in verse seventeen: 'How precious to me are your thoughts, God!' He knew from experience that God can bring revelation to an open heart, should he need to do so. And when God did one day, David was quick to repent.

Some years ago I was present at a meeting in which, with remarkable honesty and grace, the speaker shared a remarkable life story, including moments of serious failure as well as times of great blessing. The Holy Spirit spoke powerfully. During the time of personal ministry which followed, a middle-aged minister, previously unknown to me, remained sitting in his seat, the tears flowing down his face. He beckoned for me to join him and as we found a quiet place to sit, the dam broke. He was overcome with sobbing from deep inside. I laid a hand on his shoulder and waited, praying silently. When he could speak, he told me how, as a Christian teenager, he had committed a sexual act of which he was ashamed, and which had remained as a black hole under his life and ministry ever since. He had never been able to tell anyone.

We talked a little and then at his request I began to pray with him. Towards the end of my prayer he broke into the most amazing laughter. Afterwards I asked him what had been going on. He replied, 'It was one thing you said'. I had described a picture I felt God showed me, in which God was giving him a clean sheet to write the rest of his life on. He said, 'You couldn't have known, but last week I invited an experienced youth leader to come to our church and look at everything we are doing with our youth, and to advise us on the best strategy to take it forward. I said to him, "You are free to recommend anything at all – I am giving you a clean sheet".' Wiping his eyes he added, 'I never knew God could give *me* a clean sheet'.

The burden was gone. He had stepped into the light.

Writing to the Christians in Rome, Paul said, 'let us ... put on the armour of light' (Rom. 13:12). Light as armour – it's a striking thought. If I was on the battlefield, about to go over the top to confront the enemy's dug-in forces, I would like something more than daylight between me and the fiery onslaught ahead. I think part of Paul's thinking is that areas of our lives which are hidden are actually exposed to enemy fire; whereas, areas of our lives which are shared come under the protection of the work of the Spirit through the body of Christ. Someone once said, 'Either the secrecy kills the discipleship, or the discipleship kills the secrecy'. The words speak powerfully to us today. For followers of Jesus, living in the light is the safest place on earth and the touchstone of true discipleship.

6. Forgiveness

'Then Peter came to Jesus and asked, "Lord, how many times shall I forgive my brother or sister who sins against me? Up to seven times?" Jesus answered, "I tell you, not seven times, but seventy-seven times"' (Matt. 18:21–22).

'Be kind and compassionate to one another, forgiving each other, just as in Christ God forgave you' (Eph. 4:32).

When Jesus answered Peter's question about forgiveness, I don't think he meant that my brother is safe, sinning against me up to seventy-seven times, but seventy-eight and its *POW! Got you! You thought I wasn't counting!* I think he was saying, 'Peter, when it comes to forgiveness, you just keep going, the way I do – over and over and over'. I, for one, am glad that Jesus' forgiving grace never comes to an end.

When we set out to share our lives together as a community of disciples, we find friendships at various levels. Because we all make mistakes it is inevitable that forgiveness is going to be a frequent part of the equation. We won't always measure up to expectations; sometimes we will misunderstand; sometimes, consciously or unconsciously, we will offend, we will be responsible for another's hurt. The closer the relationships we desire to have, the more important it is that we keep our hearts open to forgiving grace – inbound and outbound! 'Bear with each other', said Paul, 'and forgive one another if any of you has a grievance against someone. Forgive as the Lord forgave you' (Col. 3:13).

Forgiveness is not only important to maintaining ongoing relationships; it is also the key to receiving healing where we have been damaged in the past. It may be someone who hurt us but who has never faced the truth or asked for forgiveness, or who may not even be alive today. It may be someone with whom I have attempted to be reconciled but the door has remained closed. On the cross, Jesus forgave those who neither knew what they were doing nor were remotely interested in forgiveness. Forgiveness is part of the process of our being set free from hurt or bitterness. The day I forgave my father changed the way I felt about him and it was part of a process of healing. When I truly forgive another I release them – they owe me nothing. But the first person to be released by my act of forgiveness is me.

The most helpful and practical book I have come across about forgiveness is Joff Day's *Settled Accounts: Learning How to Forgive and Release*, a valuable guide for anyone who is struggling with a practical issue.[1]

7. Loyalty

'Do not let loyalty and faithfulness forsake you; bind them around your neck, write them on the tablet of your heart. So you will find favor and good repute in the sight of God and of people' (Prov. 3:3–4, NRSV).

In today's society of betrayal, serial relationships, broken marriages and broken families, the church of Jesus has a wonderful opportunity to display in high relief the values of the kingdom of God. Faithful relationships are characterised by loyalty. Instead of scuppering a friendship, an offence becomes the occasion of fresh vulnerability and renewed commitment. Gossip dies where loyalty is at the heart of a community. Illegitimate rumour runs into a brick wall and collapses; the rumour mill itself coughs, splutters and expires for lack of oxygen.

Loyalty is when my name is safe in another's presence, whether I am present or absent. Loyalty looks after the interests of others. Loyalty chooses to believe the best and will do so through thick and thin, unless and until honourable process reveals otherwise. Promises are kept, relationships are not abandoned because they are no longer convenient. Loyalty is that aspect of love which 'always protects, always trusts, always hopes, always perseveres' (1 Cor. 13:7).

It was, perhaps, the best piece of advice in the whole of Proverbs: 'Do not let loyalty and faithfulness forsake you; bind them around your neck, write them on the tablet of your heart'. It belongs on page one of the disciple's handbook.

What if?

In Matthew 18, Jesus talked about relationships between his followers, because he knew that there would be times when, in spite of our best intentions, a relationship would run into difficulties.

> *If your brother or sister sins, go and point out their fault, just*
> *between the two of you. If they listen to you, you have won them*
> *over. But if they will not listen, take one or two others along,*
> *so that 'every matter may be established by the testimony of*
> *two or three witnesses.' If they still refuse to listen, tell it to the*

church; and if they refuse to listen even to the church, treat them as you would a pagan or a tax collector. Truly I tell you, whatever you bind on earth will be bound in heaven, and whatever you loose on earth will be loosed in heaven.

(Matt. 18:15–18)

Jesus meant us to take him seriously when he spoke of steps that might be necessary where someone simply isn't responding to help in resolving a relational breakdown. Detailed comment lies outside the purpose of this book, but perhaps two observations are appropriate.

Firstly, to be able, as a community, to lovingly walk through a process like the one Jesus outlined in Matthew 18, we would first need to have in place a growing kingdom culture. The process brings grace and truth in equal measure; it involves the presence and work of the Spirit, servant leadership and, throughout the body, humility, clarity and loving commitment. The whole end in view is redemption.

Secondly, it is a solemn thought, but where, ultimately, one party refuses to accept the faithful help of the church, there remains no basis for further fellowship – they are to be treated differently. Jesus wanted his disciples to understand that unresolved relationships are not an option in God's kingdom. It is as important as that. Our relationships are indeed intended to reflect the nature of God.

Taking stock

I have suggested that there are seven elements which constitute faithful relationships;

– Commitment

– Acceptance

– Honour

– Encouragement

– Transparency

– Forgiveness

– Loyalty

Now imagine the impact of being discipled in a church community seeking grace to live out those values in the power of the Holy Spirit. On this foundation we can build discipleship and ministry. From this foundation we can pursue our mission to proclaim Jesus! And we can tell the world of his invitation to join in the dance of creation – the community of love.

....

A culture of faithful relationships – seven elements
– reflections

For the church community

• What level of commitment do you think is reflected in your current relationships and involvement in the Church?

• Think through the seven practical elements of faithful relationships. Which do you find confirming and reassuring? Are there any which leave you feeling challenged or maybe a little threatened, or which you might want to question?

• If the Lord has spoken to you about anything in the area of openness and transparency, he would love for you to talk to him about it. His responses will always be gracious and encouraging, never condemning. He might prompt you to share it with someone else who can help.

• Is there a relationship you once had with someone (or maybe with a group) in the body of Christ, which has been broken or simply lost and which the Lord is bringing to your attention? If there is, ask him what the next step might be.

For leaders

- How do you assess the relational foundation of your church?

- In view of the instructions Jesus gave to his disciples in Matthew 18:13–18, do you agree, or disagree, with the conclusion: 'Jesus wanted his disciples to understand that unresolved relationships are not an option in the kingdom of God'?

- If you agree, are there existing areas of relational breakdown to which leadership have a responsibility to bring resolution, in ways that honour the Lord?

- What measures could the leadership put in place, by word and action, to strengthen personal relationships across your church? Are you leading by example – for instance, in the areas of openness and transparency?

[1] Joff Day, *Settled Accounts: Learning How to Forgive and Release* (Sovereign World Ltd, 1994).

Chapter Twelve
A culture of
Word and Spirit

The Scriptures and the power

Confronted one day by the Sadducees with a question about marriage and the resurrection, Jesus replied: 'You are in error because you do not know the Scriptures or the power of God' (Matt. 22:29).

In the body of Christ, our journey towards fully embracing Word and Spirit continues. The journey touches every part of the Church's life and mission and nowhere more so than the area of discipleship. Discipleship will become more and more fruitful when it is rooted in a culture where the Holy Spirit is welcomed and celebrated and the Scriptures are regularly taught as living, breathing truth.

Word and Spirit and discipleship

Word and Spirit were intertwined in Jesus' equipping of his disciples. We have already seen how he gave time and attention to teaching his disciples throughout his ministry. Then towards the end, Jesus spoke much of the Holy Spirit whom he would send to them from the Father. When they had been sent out in pairs to preach the good news of the kingdom, healing the sick and casting out demons, they had actually tasted something of the Spirit's working themselves. Jesus explained it in the upper room. Whilst the world didn't perceive or know the Spirit, he said, 'you know him, for he lives with you and will be in you' (John 14:17). The Spirit had been alongside them in their Galilean mission, enabling the miracles they performed and inspiring the words they spoke; but after Jesus' return to the Father, their experience of him would be at a deeper level still. The Spirit would live *in* them, pervading their whole being.

After the resurrection, Jesus' dual emphasis on Word and Spirit continued. On the road to Emmaus, the downcast travellers had seen the miracles, but their world had fallen apart because they didn't *understand*. So Jesus begins to enlighten them: 'beginning with Moses and all the Prophets, he explained to them what was said in all the Scriptures concerning himself' (Luke 24:27).

For forty days prior to his being taken up to heaven, he continued to instruct his disciples, often around the meal table, about the kingdom of God. But then he has more to say about the Holy Spirit:

> *Do not leave Jerusalem, but wait for the gift my Father promised, which you have heard me speak about. For John baptised with water, but in a few days you will be baptised with the Holy Spirit … you will receive power when the Holy Spirit comes on you*
>
> (Acts 1:4–5,8)

From beginning to end – the Scriptures and the power. On the Day of Pentecost, drenched in the promised Spirit, the disciples knew that the power had come. Now they were ready to go outside and proclaim the good news to the crowds in the city streets. They had the *Word*, a dynamic message of the life and death and resurrection of the Lord Jesus, the living story of events that fulfilled the ancient Scriptures so treasured by the people of Israel. And now they had the *Spirit*. Acts chapter 2 brings it together. Describing what happened that day, Luke says (in *his* Part Two):

> *All of them were filled with the Holy Spirit and began to speak in other tongues as the Spirit enabled them.*
>
> (Acts 2:4)

Then Peter stood up with the Eleven, raised his voice and addressed the crowd: 'Fellow Jews and all of you who live in Jerusalem, let me explain this to you; listen carefully to what I say ... this is what was spoken by the prophet Joel'

(Acts 2:14,16)

The disciples understood that the Word (written or proclaimed) and the Spirit belonged together. I learned it by experience that night in Bristol forty years ago, when the Spirit graciously came in new measure, releasing me into a different way of life and service. I had been fairly well versed in Scripture for some years and was blessed by that grounding (I am still grateful for it, although I realised later that I knew Scripture better than I understood it). But when the Spirit fills he opens up a new dimension, which for me was life changing. If the blood of Jesus is the *ground* of the new covenant, the Holy Spirit is the *life* of the new covenant.

When we welcome the Spirit into our church communities, actively seeking his presence and making room for him, from the leaders' meeting to the farthest corner of the church's life, we develop a culture in which disciples can grow in understanding and experience, learning to live from the Spirit within. The teaching of the Word and the ministry of the Holy Spirit combine in the process of discipleship.

Word and Spirit in the life of Jesus

1. An authentic example

Peter's first letter, written to Christians in a large area of modern-day Turkey, has much to say about suffering. In chapter 2 verse 21 he says, 'To this you were called, because Christ suffered for you, leaving you an example, that you should follow in his steps'. As in suffering, so in everything – Jesus is our example. Eugene Peterson translates: 'This is the kind of life you've been invited into, the kind of life Christ lived. He suffered everything that came his way *so you would know that it could be done, and also know how to do it, step-by-step'* (1 Pet. 2:21, *The Message*, italics mine). As we look at Jesus, we know that it is possible to live in a way that pleases God – it has been done! Jesus showed us how.

Because he is our example, we can expect to find that the Word of God and the Holy Spirit played a significant part in his own life. And so they did. During the three years the disciples spent with Jesus, they could not have missed how the Master himself was guided by the Word and dependent on the Spirit. He lived in the 'now' of the breath of God and as he did so, words spoken and written in centuries past were brought alive and fulfilled in a Spirit-filled present. Jesus lived and served as the embodiment of Scripture, soaked in its very language, empowered by the Spirit.

Speaking of the coming Messiah, Isaiah prophesied:

> *The Spirit of the LORD will rest on him – the Spirit of wisdom and of understanding, the Spirit of counsel and of might, the Spirit of the knowledge and fear of the LORD – and he will delight in the fear of the LORD.*
>
> (Isa. 11:2–3)

It wasn't just about works of power. Every aspect of Jesus' 'life on earth' (Heb. 5:7 – literally, 'the days of his flesh') was empowered by the Word and the Spirit – his obedience as well as his healing touch, his humility as well as his authority over dark powers. Having 'shared in [our] humanity' (Heb. 2:14), he lived from the very same source which is available to his followers. How else could he be called, 'the pioneer ... of *faith*' (Heb. 12:2, italics mine)? We run the race, fixing our eyes on Jesus, *because* he blazed the trail in the path of faith and won through. The more I listen to Scripture, the more I am persuaded that it was as a man, with a man's resources in God – the Word and the Spirit – that Jesus lived for God. His example is authentic.

2. His character
Following his baptism, 'Jesus, full of the Holy Spirit, left the Jordan and

was led by the Spirit into the wilderness' (Luke 4:1). Mark's description is more intense: 'At once the Spirit *sent* him out into the wilderness' (Mark 1:12, italics mine). The Holy Spirit moved Jesus quite strongly to confront the enemy. In the wilderness, Jesus faced temptation just as we do, though at a different level, and overcame the tempter on every prong of his attack. Whatever enticement away from the will of God we may face tomorrow, Jesus has defeated Satan *on that point*.

The writer to the Hebrew Christians assures us that 'we do not have a high priest who is unable to feel sympathy for our weaknesses, but we have one who has been tempted in every way, just as we are – yet he did not sin' (Heb. 4:15). The whole world was offered to him but he stayed true! Was it because he had an inside track that we could never have? I don't think so. Hebrews 2:18 shows us what temptation was like for Jesus: 'Because he himself suffered when he was tempted, he is able to help those who are being tempted.' It wasn't a pretend temptation and it wasn't a pretend victory.

Matthew's narrative indicates how important the Word of God was to Jesus and how powerfully he used it to overcome Satan. Resisting the enemy's attacks, Jesus replies three times, 'It is written … It is written … It is written'.

> *Jesus answered, 'It is written: "Man shall not live on bread alone, but on every word that comes from the mouth of God."'*
>
> **(Matt. 4:4, quoting Deut. 8:3)**

> *Jesus answered him, 'It is also written: "Do not put the Lord your God to the test."'*
>
> **(Matt. 4:7, quoting Deut. 6:16)**

> *Jesus said to him, 'Away from me, Satan! For it is written: "Worship the Lord your God, and serve him only."'*
>
> **(Matt. 4:10, quoting Deut. 6:13)**

The Word of God had been stored up in his heart and mind during the Nazareth years. It lived in him. Now, under intense pressure in the wilderness, it is the written Word, quickened by the Spirit, which frames his thoughts and responses. It became the sword in his hand, defeating the enemy.

Luke's narrative emphasises the part played by the Holy Spirit. The temptation of Jesus is *preceded* by the account of his anointing with the Spirit at his baptism (Chapter 3). It is *introduced* with the words, 'Jesus, full of the Holy Spirit, left the Jordan and was led by the Spirit into the wilderness' (Luke 4:1). It *concludes*: 'Jesus returned to Galilee in the power of the Spirit' (Luke 4:14).

We can hardly miss the implication. It was as a man filled with the Spirit, with the Word of God in his heart, that Jesus passed through the wilderness experience. He really was the pioneer of faith. Clark Pinnock put it this way: '[the] Spirit enabled Jesus to live within the limits of human nature during his life ... Through obedience to the Father and dependence on the Spirit, the Son of God recapitulated humanity's history. He reversed the human no that led to our fallenness and returned the yes that was the divine purpose for humanity.'[1]

Perhaps this is part of what Paul described when he talks about how Jesus 'made himself nothing' (Phil. 2:7). He 'emptied' himself, voluntarily becoming dependent on the Spirit. The power of this for us today is that Jesus' life is not only our example – it opens a door of hope for you and me! Disciples are invited to follow him with the help of the same Spirit, guided by the same Word.

Commenting on this verse, F.F. Bruce recalls the words spoken to Jesus on the cross. Pointing in ridicule at the figure hanging there helpless, his tormentors said, 'He trusts in God', unaware of just how true that was! Bruce comments, 'It was sheer faith in God, unsupported by any visible or tangible evidence, that carried him through the taunting, the scourging, the crucifying, and the more bitter agony of rejection, desertion, and dereliction'.[2]

His whole life was shaped by the Word and enabled by the Spirit.

He was the dependent man.

3. His ministry

At Jesus' baptism in the River Jordan, the Spirit comes upon him, anointing him for his mission: 'And as he was praying, heaven was opened and the Holy Spirit descended on him in bodily form like a dove' (Luke 3:21–22). He performed miracles, not because he was the Son of God, but as a man filled with the Holy Spirit. He was able to heal because God's presence was with him.

> *You know what has happened throughout the province of Judea ... how God anointed Jesus of Nazareth with the Holy Spirit and power ... [who] went around doing good and healing all who were under the power of the devil, because God was with him.*
>
> **(Acts 10:37–38)**

Jesus said later that he drove out demons by the Spirit of God (Matt. 12:28).

As to the Word, shortly after his baptism, Jesus stood in the synagogue at Nazareth with Scripture in his hand, announcing his calling and ministry:

> *The Spirit of the Lord is on me, because he has anointed me to proclaim good news to the poor. He has sent me to proclaim freedom for the prisoners and recovery of sight for the blind, to set the oppressed free, to proclaim the year of the Lord's favour.*
>
> **(Luke 4:18–19, quoting Isa. 61:1–2)**

His ministry flowed consciously from the prophetic Word, under the Spirit's anointing.

4. His sacrifice

The sacrifice of Jesus at the cross also fulfilled the Word. The cross may have been veiled in unusual darkness, but in another sense, it stood in the blazing light of 'all that the prophets have spoken' (Luke 24:25), bringing to completion so much of the symbol and promise of Scripture. The writer to the Hebrews draws on Psalm 40 (vv6–8) to explain to his readers what was going on in the heart of the incarnate Jesus.

> *Therefore, when Christ came into the world, he said: … 'Here I am – it is written about me in the scroll – I have come to do your will, my God.'*
>
> **(Heb. 10:5–7)**

The life and ministry of Jesus sprang from his delight in doing his Father's will. To the psalmist, the scroll would have referred to the Torah, the first five books of the Bible, but the writer to the Hebrews might well have been thinking of the Old Testament as a whole. The *law* contained the will of God for human kind – loving him with heart and soul and mind and strength, and our neighbours as ourselves, all of which was fulfilled in Jesus. God's law was within his heart. The *prophetic scriptures* were about the coming Messiah, whose perfect life would be offered up in sacrifice. He would suffer, rise again and be exalted as Saviour and King, to bring salvation to Jews and Gentiles: 'it is written about me in the scroll' (Heb. 10:7).

So much was written before Jesus came – so much was in his heart as he went to the cross. To Peter in the garden, his blood-spattered sword still grasped at the ready, Jesus said, 'Put your sword back in its place … Do you think I cannot call on my Father, and he will at once put at my disposal more than twelve legions of angels? *But how then would the Scriptures be fulfilled* that say it must happen in this way?' (Matt. 26:52–54, italics mine).

We rarely talk about it, but the cross involved the Spirit, too. It is truly awesome to think that the Holy Spirit helped Jesus to submit to the Father's will and to endure the cross. 'How much more, then', says the writer to the Hebrews, 'will the blood of Christ, who *through the eternal Spirit* offered himself unblemished to God, cleanse our consciences …

so that we may serve the living God!' (Heb. 9:14, italics mine). What can we say? We can only worship.

Word and Spirit characterised and energised the Person of Jesus, our forerunner and example. Now he invites us to follow him with our hand in his.

Word and Spirit in the church community

I find that the example of Jesus and his disciples is a challenge for church leaders and churches alike. My first appeal would be that in this era of ever smaller, 'bite-sized' communications and quick-fire images, we do not lose the capacity or desire to engage with the teaching of Scripture. The challenge for leaders is about opening up Scripture in ways that are life-giving and relevant.

For the church community as a whole, can we make the reading of Scripture (Old and New Testaments), with time for meditation and prayer, a regular part of our lives, allowing the Holy Spirit to bring revelation, guidance and that sense of wonder that leads us to worship? In the challenges of life, the Spirit cannot 'bring to mind' what we haven't read or heard in the first place. Let's feed on the living Word of God! It is part of the disciple's strength and equipping for mission.

And in every area of church life, we will continually seek the presence and refreshing of the Holy Spirit, our friend and our life-source. As we aspire to follow Jesus and to disciple others, we can only rely on the Spirit's anointing.

Prophetic words

Alongside hearing God speak to us through Scripture, he has provided for us to hear him speaking through prophetic gifts – the Spirit's words through (frail) human lips.

Among the gifts the Spirit distributes generously to the body of Christ, prophecy is especially to be desired, said Paul. Writing to the Corinthian church about spiritual gifts (Chapters 12–14) he summed up his instruction like this: 'Follow the way of love and eagerly desire gifts of the Spirit, especially prophecy' (1 Cor. 14:1).

We can be sure that prophetic words, truly prompted by the Holy Spirit, will always be in tune with the written Word. When we prophesy, God uses us to encourage one another and build each other up. Sometimes, prophecy can be predictive, confirming a path we should take, or opening up new horizons. If the Spirit is speaking of things to which God is calling us in the future, it is even more important that safeguards are in place, so that what is spoken can be weighed responsibly and appropriately endorsed by those with the maturity to do so.

Part of discipleship is learning how to respond to prophecy. Imagine you are excited after receiving a prophetic word. It has indicated new things that God has for you in days to come. The word has been weighed and affirmed – there is a clear sense that God has spoken. What happens next? Let me tell you about a little house in Japan.

A little house in Japan

On one occasion, Gerald Coates, the founder of the Pioneer network of churches and ministries in the UK, gave me just such a word. He began by saying, 'I see you in a little house in Japan,' and went on to enlarge on what God was saying. At the time I had no specific interest in Japan and certainly no thought of visiting that country, but knowing Gerald's track record in the prophetic, I began to pray about it. Nine months later, quite unconnected, another prophetic ministry, Martin Scott, came to me and said, 'You are going to Japan'. I began to think there was a risk that God was in it! I prayed about it with a renewed sense of purpose.

A year passed, then another year and another year, with no sign of anything that looked remotely like an invitation to Japan. I am sorry to say that, by then, life had moved on and the prophetic word had slipped on to the back burner; in fact, to be honest, after four years I think it had fallen off the back burner, too. A few months later I was at a Pioneer Leaders' Conference at a holiday camp in the middle of a cold English February (think well before you rush to pack!). In the late afternoon of the first day we were invited to get into groups of five and share where we were at – our challenges, our hopes, our aspirations, whatever. Sitting in that group of five, I was reminded of the word God had spoken about Japan. The Holy Spirit whispered that it hadn't been a good idea to let it go. I went back to my chalet and knelt down by the bed. I said, 'Lord, please forgive me for allowing your word to fall by the wayside'. Then I added, 'If you are still up for this, will you confirm it before I go to bed tonight' (God has to work harder with some of us than with others!).

Later, I went to the dining room for the evening meal and found myself sitting next to a young man I had never met or heard of. He was Japanese, his father led a church in Osaka and he had come to England especially for the conference. Six months later I was in Japan as part of a team of three, ministering in two churches. During our stay, a delightful pastor took us to his tiny home to meet his family, where we were honoured by being invited to participate in a Japanese tea ceremony. I thought, 'This is the "little house" Gerald saw five years ago'.

God had been very gracious – he didn't give up on the word he had spoken, even though my response had faltered. Other times I think I did better. The Lord appreciates it when we hold through proactively to see his word fulfilled.

God speaks to us in different ways: most often it is the inner voice of the Spirit; at other times he speaks through another's counsel. Sometimes God speaks to us in a dream, or through a member of the body with the gift of prophecy; and sometimes through Scripture. Word and Spirit complement each other.

Come Holy Spirit! Flood our lives, our communities and our relationships with your presence. Speak and be heard! Fan into flame our desire to follow the Master closely and empower us to be more like him and serve him, for the sake of his name and his kingdom!

Come Holy Spirit! You inspired Scripture when it was written; you illuminate Scripture when we read it; you apply Scripture to our hearts and lives; and through your power, the Word is made flesh in us, too, when we yield to the Lord Jesus Christ.

Discipleship flourishes in a culture of Word and Spirit.

A culture of Word and Spirit – *reflections*

For the church community

- In what ways do the Word and the Spirit connect with your everyday life?

- Does your desire to become more like Jesus lead you to open your heart and mind to the Scriptures regularly, inviting the Holy Spirit to bring God's Word alive and make it part of you, as it was of Jesus?

- If you are experienced in one or more of the gifts of the Spirit, how would you like to see this develop?

- Meditate on Jesus as our complete and real example, showing us the way in everything. Allow the Holy Spirit to bring fresh encouragement and new faith.

- If you are part of a group, ask the Holy Spirit together to come now and fill you. If you are reading this alone, why not pause and do the same.

For leaders

- How do you understand what Scripture has to say about Word and Spirit in relation to the humanity of Jesus? What does it mean for you?

- What excites you and what concerns you about your church's current experience of 'the Scriptures and the power'? If God was to speak about your church's direction, what might he want to say?

- How are the gifts of the Spirit operating in your church? Is there enough space for them to grow?

- Is this a moment to look behind your ministry and ask yourself – how am I doing in my own experience of the spiritual disciplines of worship, prayer, fasting and Scripture; and in my experience of the Holy Spirit? That is a conversation between you and the Lord. It is the outcomes that will be seen by others.

[1] Clark H. Pinnock, *Flame of Love* (InterVarsity Press, 1996) pp88,98.

[2] F.F. Bruce, *The Epistle to the Hebrews, Revised, The New International Commentary on the New Testament* (Eerdmans, 1990) p338.

Chapter Thirteen

A culture of seeking after God

God seekers

The true disciple is a seeker after God; God is our ultimate passion. When Jesus returns and finally hands over the kingdom to God the Father, it is 'that God may be all in all' (1 Cor. 15:28).

Writing to the Ephesian Christians in the very city where the famous temple of Artemis was located, Paul described God's people as joined together in Christ, 'to become a holy temple in the Lord … a dwelling in which God lives by his Spirit' (Eph. 2:21–22). Ordinary Christians, filled with the Spirit, hosting among them the presence of the living God!

For the local church, the presence of God is our passion and our validation – God making himself known in our worship, our prayer, our ministry to one another and our mission; revealing himself in supernatural ways. When the church community has set its heart on pursuing God's presence, discipleship is set on its magnetic north. We are on course when we are being discipled in a culture of seeking after God – his face, his glory, his healing presence. Martin Nystrom's beautiful song echoes the psalmist:

> *As the deer pants for the water,*
> *So my soul longs after You;*
> *You alone are my heart's desire*
> *And I long to worship You.*[1]

It is the language of the tryst, the language of intimacy. As I write this, I recall an occasion only a few weeks ago, in our home church in Chipping Campden, Gloucestershire. We were experiencing the felt presence of God and a worship leader quietly led us into this song. It was a memorable moment as the song released to God what was in our hearts. It seemed like there was a corporate intimacy with him, as tears flowed and lives were touched. Discipleship flourishes in the presence of God.

Our experience of God's presence as churches flows from our personal walk with God. What we experience of God in our daily lives and in the quiet place of communion, we bring into the gathered community. When spirit joins with spirit under the leadership of the Holy Spirit, God comes among his people and the temple fills with the fragrance of worship.

Keeping it simple

Each of us has a unique relationship with Jesus. I find that special moments arise in the simplest of ways. My quiet place at home to worship and pray is a chair in the sitting room, looking towards the patio doors and the garden. One morning, I began to open my heart to the Lord. As I waited on him, from 'nowhere' the four lines of a hymn I hadn't sung for decades came to mind:

> *Loved with everlasting love,*
> *Led by grace that love to know*
> *Spirit breathing from above,*
> *Thou hast have taught me it is so.*[2]

The old fashioned words seemed to have new meaning. For a while I just enjoyed his love – love that would never end and yet was passionate every morning. Eventually, I turned to the passages in my reading plan for that day. The first was from the Old Testament and there it was – jumping out at me from Jeremiah 31:3: 'I have loved you with an everlasting love'.

Sometimes the Lord and I have these moments – I expect you do, too. You can't really describe them to anybody else. In the Song of Solomon the bride says: 'His words are kisses, his kisses words' (Songs 5:16, *The Message*). That comes close.

Whatever stage we are at in the Christian life, whether we are new Christians or have been on the road for a long time, we can all seek after God. It is the simple longing of hearts that love him, giving time and space to our Eternal Lover.

Day-to-day relationship

During their three years with the Master, the twelve disciples had the privilege of observing many things about Jesus' lifestyle. One of the most striking must surely have been the recurring evidence of his relationship with God. It breathed through his aspect, his peace, his attitudes; through his words and actions, and especially through his praying. Prayer was at the heart of his oneness with his Father. For Jesus, prayer expressed the orientation of a life sourced in God and centred on God. Conversation flowed out of communion.

Isaiah painted a prophetic picture of the coming Servant. Isaiah's simple words give us a glimpse of how each day started for Jesus, the Servant of God:

> *The Lord GOD has given me the tongue of a teacher, that I*
> *may know how to sustain the weary with a word. Morning*
> *by morning he wakens—wakens my ear to listen as those*
> *who are taught. The Lord GOD has opened my ear ...*
> *The Lord GOD helps me ... he who vindicates me is near.*
> (Isa. 50:4–5,7–8, NRSV)

In those times of listening and prayer, Jesus received from his Father words for that day. His ear and his heart were open, and the awareness of God's presence and help remained with him through the day ahead.

Jesus' prayer journey in Luke's Gospel

Some remarkable moments in the relationship between Jesus and his Father were witnessed by the disciples in the prayer recorded in John 17 and in the Gethsemane prayers. Suffering and surrender, heart-cry and yieldedness, flowed together in the real-life incense of worship and trust.

But it is Luke who gives us the fullest picture of the day-to-day relationship with God in prayer, which characterised Jesus from the beginning. Once again we will find that Jesus is our example, not to make us feel small or inadequate, much less condemned – he simply isn't like that – but to encourage us as we take the next step on our personal journey. His grace holds the door open, with a smile that warms and beckons us at the same time. Let's look at the recorded moments in Jesus' prayer journey, as Luke describes them.

Luke is the only gospel writer who tells us that after Jesus had been baptised, he came up out of the water and was praying. And while he prayed, the Spirit fell:

> *When all the people were being baptised, Jesus was baptised too. And as he was praying, heaven was opened and the Holy Spirit descended on him in bodily form like a dove. And a voice came from heaven: 'You are my Son, whom I love; with you I am well pleased.'*

> **(Luke 3:21–22)**

In the experience of obedience and prayer and being anointed with the Spirit, Jesus heard the Father's spoken affirmation of love and approval. His ministry flowed out of union with God.

Jesus, full of the Holy Spirit, left the Jordan and was led by the Spirit into the wilderness, where for forty days he was tempted by the devil. He ate nothing during those days, and at the end of them he was hungry. The devil said to him, 'If you are the Son of God, tell this stone to become bread.' Jesus answered, 'It is written: "Man shall not live on bread alone."'

(Luke 4:1–4)

During those days of fasting, Jesus was waiting on God, living, not by bread, but by the Word of God. What he drew from the Father strengthened him in the hour of testing.

But Jesus often withdrew to lonely places and prayed.

(Luke 5:16)

I can hear the disciples saying, 'Has anyone seen Jesus this morning?' And they would all know where he was. Those frequent times of private prayer were the bedrock of his daily life and the source of everything that happened in the public place.

One of those days Jesus went out to a mountainside to pray, and spent the night praying to God. When morning came, he called his disciples to him and chose twelve of them, whom he also designated apostles

(Luke 6:12–13)

There were important choices to be made in the day ahead which would be strategic for the kingdom. Jesus spent the whole night alone with his Father. During those hours, he received guidance about whom he should choose to be with him from that time on, for personal discipling.

Once when Jesus was praying in private and his disciples
were with him, he asked them, 'Who do the crowds say I am?'
They replied, 'Some say John the Baptist; others say Elijah;
and still others, that one of the prophets of long ago has come
back to life.' 'But what about you?' he asked. 'Who do you say
I am?' Peter answered, 'God's Messiah.'

(Luke 9:18–20)

Out of Jesus' prayers came Peter's public confession of the revelation God had given him. Father and Son were acting as one.

About eight days after Jesus said this, he took Peter, John
and James with him and went up onto a mountain to pray.
As he was praying, the appearance of his face changed, and
his clothes became as bright as a flash of lightning.

(Luke 9:28–29)

The Transfiguration occurred during a prayer time with three of his disciples. Peter, James and John found themselves under an open heaven, with Jesus, seeing and hearing new things. The more we read, the more it seems that everything flowed out of Jesus' communion with his Father.

One day Jesus was praying in a certain place. When he
finished, one of his disciples said to him, 'Lord, teach us
to pray, just as John taught his disciples.' He said to them,
'When you pray, say: "Father"'

(Luke 11:1–2)

It was watching Jesus at prayer that prompted the disciples to ask him to teach them to pray, too. The very first words of Jesus' reply showed them that an intimate relationship with the Father was open to them also.

*Simon, Simon, Satan has asked to sift all of you as wheat. But
I have prayed for you, Simon, that your faith may not fail.*

(Luke 22:31–32)

During those times of praying alone, Peter had been one of the people
Jesus talked to God about. And God heard him. Over and over, Luke draws
our attention to Jesus' communion with God – it was central to his whole
life and ministry. It was day-to-day; it flowed naturally through everything.

The furnace of fire

'When he rose from prayer' (Luke 22:45).

When Jesus rose from prayer in Gethsemane it was to go to the cross. The
same relationship with God that had sustained him every day held true
at the time of his deepest suffering. Even on the cross, God was still his
true centre, from the prayer for the forgiveness of his persecutors, to the
moment when he plumbed the depths – 'my God, why … ?' (Matt. 27:46).

When the sacrifice was complete and victory secure, his final
words were, 'Father, into your hands I commit my spirit' (Luke 23:46).
Dismissing his spirit was a leap into the realm of death with his hand in
his Father's and his face towards God, as it had been all his life.

We can only look at him with awe and wonder, yet his grace and love
draw us on to seek after God. Our hearts respond: 'Here we are in our
weakness – sometimes forgetful, sometimes distracted by our busyness;
but we do love you. We want to be more like Jesus, experiencing more
of your presence, in the secret place and in the ups and downs of life.'

Be encouraged! Jeremiah didn't say, 'His demands are new every
morning' – he said, 'his compassions … are new every morning'
(Lam. 3:22–23). No wonder he added: 'I say to myself, "The LORD is my
portion; therefore I will wait for him." The LORD is good to those whose
hope is in him, to the one who seeks him' (vv24–25).

Seeking after God in community

To think of seeking after God as a personal pursuit only would be to miss the whole purpose of the salvation story. This is how David expressed his constant longing:

> *One thing I ask from the LORD, this only do I seek: that I may dwell in the house of the LORD all the days of my life, to gaze on the beauty of the LORD and to seek him in his temple.*

> **(Psa. 27:4)**

Salvation is not individualistic and neither is discipleship. We noted at the beginning of this chapter that, as a community of disciples, we *are* 'the house of the Lord'. In his living temple we seek the presence of God *together*; we pray *together*; we worship *together*; through Jesus, we have a corporate relationship with God. God is at the centre of our shared lives. That is where a whole salvation is found – in community, not in independence.

In a culture of seeking after God we can be discipled and disciple others. And those who find faith, born into the family of God by the Spirit, find themselves pointed towards God by everything around them, and their lives oriented Godwards.

Jesus and fasting

John's disciples were scratching their heads. John the Baptist had led an ascetic lifestyle, neither eating bread nor drinking wine (see Matt. 11:18–19), and his followers fasted regularly. The Pharisees also fasted, twice a week – Mondays and Thursdays. Observing Jesus and his disciples eating and drinking (not to mention the unlikely people with whom they sometimes shared a table), they asked Jesus why his disciples didn't fast the way they did. His reply was significant: 'How can the guests of the bridegroom mourn while he is with them?' (Matt. 9:15).

The King was here and it was a time of joy and celebration – prodigals were returning and being blessed and there was a party going on around Jesus. He said the time would come when he would be taken away – then they would fast.

Given that, for the Pharisees, the most important thing about fasting was being noticed, Jesus had already taught his disciples in the Sermon on the Mount that fasting was for the Father to see (see Matt. 6:16–18). Scripture gives us one notable instance of Jesus fasting – the forty days without food in the wilderness, before his public ministry began. There are striking analogies between Jesus' experience in the wilderness and the testing of Israel some 1,300 years before. Both occurred in the wilderness. The forty days for Jesus corresponded to the forty years for Israel. The responses of Jesus to the three temptations are all taken from the Deuteronomy review of Israel's desert days (see Deut. 6:13,16; 8:3).

But whereas Israel failed tests of obedience over and over again, Jesus emerged from the wilderness, fully dependent on God, fully devoted and fully trusting. Israel had grieved the Holy Spirit (see Isa. 63:10); Jesus came through the experience filled with the Spirit and guided by the Spirit, from beginning to end. He was all that God's people had failed to be. His inner life was centred on God, and fasting had been an expression of that.

Scripture doesn't mention Jesus fasting privately during his ministry.[3] He may well have done. His words to his disciples at the well in Samaria certainly demonstrate the spirit of it:

> '*I have food to eat that you know nothing about.*' *Then his disciples said to each other, 'Could someone have brought him food?' 'My food,' said Jesus, 'is to do the will of him who sent me and to finish his work.*'
>
> (John 4:32–34)

If the *Word of God,* rather than food, sustained him in the wilderness, *doing the will of God* sustained him at the well. His entire being terminated on God; accomplishing the Father's will was everything.

Christianity Today invited three American Christian leaders to answer the question, 'What classic spiritual discipline needs the most renewal among American Christians?' In his contribution, Jonathan Wilson-Hartgrove said this:

> *We are often consumed by anxiety about image, fear about the future, and desires for cheap comfort and instant gratification. A thousand forces conspire to distract us from our truest desires every day. For this reason, I'm convinced that fasting is the spiritual discipline we most need to renew today … Those who learn to hunger and thirst for righteousness are blessed because they will be filled – not with the cheap comfort of the passing moment, but with the true Bread that satisfies.*[4]

I believe God is speaking to us about seeking him with prayer and fasting. As often observed, Jesus' instruction of his disciples about fasting began with the words, 'When you fast' – not 'if'. There is also a place for fasting by the community as a whole. There will be times for calling God's people to unite in prayer and fasting for a shorter or longer period; seasons of the Spirit when a corporate seeking after God, with fasting, is the response that will release his purposes.

Learning the grace lesson again

Spiritual disciplines, such as prayer and fasting, are a special target of the enemy because he knows their potential. His strategy is straightforward – lose them or legalise them. And that's the real killer. Getting up in the morning with a list of twenty things I must do today to be a good Christian is like putting on a 50kg backpack before I start out! I learned through failure and sometimes success that prayer and fasting flow, not from great ideas and good intentions, but from enjoying the Father's grace. It is resting in his love that kindles the fire of affection and desire.

In the mid-nineties, when the recent outpouring of the Spirit was still fresh in the experience of many UK churches, prophetic voices were talking about seeking God's face through prayer and fasting. I remember hearing a humble testimony from a servant of God as he described the experience of fasting for forty days, seeking God's presence. I came away inspired with a vision of drawing near to God in a dimension I hadn't known before. I had fasted for various periods of time but nothing like I heard that night.

Eventually, I chose a day and set myself to fast from food for forty days. It all seemed to begin well, but after a week I was finding it hard going on every level. After eleven days, what had been in my heart seemed to have evaporated and I abandoned the fast with a sense of disappointment. I wasn't exactly feeling like God's man of the hour!

At the time I was part of the national leadership team of Pioneer, then led by Gerald Coates. A few months later, as the Holy Spirit continued to move, there was a prayerful and prophetic call in the team (and for leaders throughout the network) to fast in some way for a twenty-five-day period that lay between two Pioneer events. The consensus and the level of response suggested that God was in it, and indeed he was.

Having recovered from the previous disappointment, I responded wholeheartedly and, looking back over my journal, they were for me remarkable days of knowing more of God's presence and love. Even physically, after the first few days of going without food, it became easier. At the end of the twenty-five days, I was surprised to find that I really didn't want to stop. Through God's mercy and kindness I was enjoying something new with him and I wanted more. At the end of forty days, there was a sense of peace that the fast was complete. On the last day, I wrote in my journal the words of Jeremiah 15:16: 'When your words came, I ate them; they were my joy and my heart's delight'.

At the time, Muriel and I lived in Nottinghamshire and the following day we went to a country farm and craft centre with a small restaurant.

I ordered a modest dish of bacon and mushrooms on toast and a glass of red wine. It tasted special. God had given me an opportunity to learn the grace lesson again. It is summed up in what God said to the people of Judah through the prophet Zechariah: 'And I will pour out on the house of David and the inhabitants of Jerusalem a spirit of grace and supplication' (Zech. 12:10).

Grace and supplication! There it was. When God gives a spirit of grace along with the desire to seek him, it's different.

I share the story because it illustrates that spiritual disciplines of any kind flow, not from the 'must do' that arises from some kind of pressure – it just doesn't work that way – but from the never ending grace of God. The God who understands our weaknesses and forgives our shortcomings is ready to draw near to us.

> *As the deer pants for the water,*
> *So my soul longs after You;*
> *You alone are my heart's desire*
> *And I long to worship You.*

Lord Jesus, take us by the hand and lead us to the Father! Teach us to live for your presence, your kingdom, and your glory. Together, as a community of disciples, with the Spirit's help, we will seek after God.

As always, learning as we go.

....

A culture of seeking after God – *reflections*

For the church community
- How do you respond to the story of Jesus' prayer journey? Do you think along the lines of, 'That's another planet' – or do you find a fresh desire rising in your heart to take the next step in your own journey of seeking after God?

- If God's kindness and grace is releasing you from a sense of pressure, or condemnation, as you read and meditate, would you like to ask the Holy Spirit to help you find a new way forward? God loves spending time with you because he loves *you*. Ask him how he would like you to respond.

- What kind of feelings are evoked when fasting is mentioned? Is it already an area of blessing and fruitfulness in your walk with God, or is it something the Holy Spirit would like to restore to a place it used to have in your life? For you, it may even be something to consider for the first time, to pray about and perhaps begin with a small step?

- If you love God, why not find a quiet place, look up into his face and tell him? Ask him to draw you into a more intimate relationship with him, through Jesus. And just worship.

For leaders

- As leaders, when we read a chapter like this, there is a temptation to think first of how one's church is doing, rather than of how it is with us. Is there anything God may be saying to you about the priorities in your own life and your journey of intimacy with him?

- If the church members were asked to identify the church's core activity, what do you think they might say?
  Worship and prayer
  Teaching and ministry
  Social action/mission

- If the presence of God is the *sine qua non* ('without which nothing') of the Church's calling and mission, are there steps you could take to encourage the church community in seeking after God?

- Do you see a place for prayer and fasting by the community as a whole? How might it come about?

---

[1] Martin Nystrom, *As the Deer* (Restoration Music Ltd, 1984).

[2] G. Wade Robinson, *I am His*, *Redemption Hymnal, Music Edition* (Marshall Morgan and Scott Ltd).

[3] In the case of Matthew 17:21 and Mark 9:29, 'This kind [of demon] can come out only by prayer and fasting', most commentators agree that the words 'and fasting' were not in the original text. The fact that they were added later says something about the understanding of Jesus and fasting in the Early Church.

[4] *Christianity Today*, March 2013.

Chapter Fourteen
A culture of servant leadership

Leading the way

You knew it, didn't you? Sooner or later we would get to the connection between kingdom culture and church leadership. The question is simple but significant. What kind of leadership will we need in order to facilitate in the local church the model of discipleship Jesus showed us in his Masterclass? The answer calls out to us from everything Jesus said and did.

First – the kind who have walked the walk. They have themselves been discipled and continue to display a teachable spirit. Second – they have servant leadership written on their hearts by the Master's hand. And third – they are passionate about empowering and releasing every single member of the body. So it's time to knock gently on the door of the church leaders' weekly meeting and ask: 'Can we have a chat about how we move forward?'

The nature of power in the kingdom of God

Some biblical guidelines will help us. The kingdom of God is not a democracy and neither is the church. Democracy is not the issue – the issue is the nature of power. We need leadership in the church, leaders who have been genuinely released to lead. But what kind of leadership represents the spirit of Jesus?

I find it helps to begin with the bigger picture. The nature of power reared its head as an issue in the Garden of Eden and was settled at the cross. More often than not, the history of nations has been the story of the pursuit and abuse of power. The seventh chapter of Daniel is central to the book and has a significant message about the nature of God's kingdom. The chapter begins with a remarkable picture of world powers and ends with a vision of Jesus that could not be in sharper contrast. The four beasts which 'came up out of the sea' (Dan. 7:3) represent four successive earthly empires. Out of the swirling currents of the enemy's activity and influence, historical empires emerge. Their source is in the unseen realm. They are pictured as beasts because they reflect the nature of the dark powers behind them. They plunder and devour because they are inspired and sourced from a kingdom that plunders and devours.

As the Old Testament era moved towards the Christ event, evil rose up, organising itself in human power structures to exert influence and gain territorial control. Since the advent of Jesus, the history of the last two thousand years has thrown up more of the same. Spiritual forces lie behind human solidarities that work against the kingdom of God. The story of nations and political leaders is full of examples where national leaders have been significantly motivated by dark powers. Control through acquisition, oppression and injustice are hallmarks.

At the heart of it all is the spirit of empire, which stems directly from the prince of this world. Satan's original rebellion against God was about creating his own empire, setting aside the rule of God. The spirit of empire is the very antithesis of the kingdom of God and our own nation's history has not been free of it. The spirit of empire can still manifest itself in society at large, whether in politics, in boardroom battles, in global corporations or in regional wars.

Tragically, after Constantine in the fourth century, the spirit of empire invaded the church of Jesus Christ, leading to the creation of religious power centres with worldly trappings to match. It has been a long road back to the simplicity that is in Christ, but we are getting there! There are signs everywhere of the renewing work of the Spirit, which we celebrate with humility and joy.

What stands in contrast to the spirit of empire is the spirit of Jesus. After the incident with the mother of James and John, when she asked Jesus to give her two sons the top spots in the kingdom, he called his disciples together and said:

> *You've observed how godless rulers throw their weight around, how quickly a little power goes to their heads. It's not going to be that way with you. Whoever wants to be great must become a servant. Whoever wants to be first among you must be your slave. That is what the Son of Man has done: He came to serve, not be served—and then to give away his life in exchange for the many who are held hostage.*
>
> **(Matt. 20:25–28, *The Message*)**

Graham Kendrick called him 'the Servant King' – a King who said, 'I am gentle and humble in heart' (Matt. 11:29), a King who wept when he saw others suffering; a King who seeks a relationship of love, not of mastery and control. Paul tells us that this King 'made himself nothing by taking the very nature of a servant, being made in human likeness. And being found in appearance as a man, he humbled himself by becoming obedient to death – even death on a cross!' (Phil. 2:7–8). These are the values at stake on the battleground of this cosmic war. The spirit of Jesus stands against the spirit of empire.

Significantly, in Revelation 14:4, the 'overcomers' of Revelation 2 and 3 (KJV) are those who 'follow the Lamb wherever he goes'. They live in the same spirit of humility and sacrificial love. Those words must have reminded John on the Isle of Patmos of what Jesus had said from the start: 'I am sending you out like lambs among wolves' (Luke 10:3). The early disciples went out, vulnerable, serving, offering healing love and sharing good news. We represent a different kind of kingdom.

Philippians 2 shows us God's response to the obedience of Jesus: 'Therefore, God exalted him to the highest place' (Phil. 2:9). That's how it works in God's kingdom: 'humility comes before honour' (Prov. 18:12).

When John finally got to see God's appointed ruler arriving at the throne, I think he got a surprise. What he saw was 'a Lamb, looking as if it had been slain' (Rev. 5:6). Power passed into the hands of sacrificial love. Here was the one man God could trust with ultimate authority on earth and in heaven. That is why Daniel 7 goes on to introduce the Son of Man and then tells us: 'He approached the Ancient of Days and was led into his presence. He was given authority, glory and sovereign power' (Dan. 7:13–14).

When authority passes into the hands of God's chosen King, it isn't taken – it is given. There lies the quantum difference between human empires and God's kingdom. And there we see the true nature of power in the kingdom of Jesus – it is power to lay down our lives, power to serve, power to love, power to give of ourselves on behalf of others. Jesus has absolute power over all flesh, but his nature is self-giving love and we need not fear. Jesus redeemed power itself.

That is why in ministry we don't set out on a career path or work to promote our own advancement. We serve in those things that God graciously gives us and our brothers and sisters lovingly endorse. True spiritual authority can only flow out of who and what we are in God – that's the real measure of it. When that is recognised by others we are given a place. True leadership is not about authority to make decisions – it is about influence and an authority to serve. This is the nature of the kingdom of which we are. In our time and place we carry the values of the Servant King.

This brings us back to leadership in the church and the question with which we began. What kind of leadership will we need in order to facilitate across the local church the kind of discipleship which emerges from Jesus' Masterclass? And the answer is – *that kind*!

Servant leadership and discipleship

Nowhere is it more important that leaders carry a servant heart than in the area of personally discipling others and overseeing the development of discipleship across the church community. To be entrusted with responsibility for influencing another's life is a huge privilege and one which we can only carry with a meekness of spirit and gentleness of word. True spiritual authority always honours the body of Christ, always profoundly respects the individual. This is no place for the tiniest vestige of a controlling spirit or an authoritarian attitude.

It is instructive to look at the atmosphere in which spiritual authority operates in the New Testament and in particular, how Paul exercised the authority he had been given.

Notice the language he uses to describe how he behaved.

> For you know that we dealt with each of you as a father
> deals with his own children, encouraging, comforting and
> urging you to live lives worthy of God, who calls you into his
> kingdom and glory.
>
> (1 Thess. 2:11–12)

> By the humility and gentleness of Christ, I appeal to you
>
> (2 Cor. 10:1)

> I speak as to wise men; you judge what I say.
>
> (1 Cor. 10:15, NASB)

This latter example is remarkable. The Corinthian church had all sorts of problems, from pride, to a divisive spirit, to immorality, all of which he addresses; but here he gives dignity to his readers, expressing trust in their ability to weigh what he says and come to right conclusions.

> And the Lord's servant must not be quarrelsome but must
> be kind to everyone, able to teach, not resentful. Opponents
> must be gently instructed
>
> (2 Tim. 2:24–25)

I am writing this not to shame you but to warn you as my dear children.

(1 Cor. 4:14)

There was always honour and respect. We find him approaching individuals with the same sensitivity, as in the example of Philemon:

I didn't want you to be kind because you had to but because you wanted to.

(Philem. 14, TLB)

There is the very heart of the new covenant. As far back as the sixteenth century, the Anabaptist leader, Menno Simons, understood the nature of spiritual authority in the body of Christ. His words deserve a moment's meditation:

Spiritual authority is never to make the rebel conform: its only purpose is to enable the obedient person to live a holy life. Therefore it rests upon obedience and submission freely given. Furthermore, spiritual authority has only spiritual means at its disposal: its only weapons are prayer, scripture, counsel and the power of a holy life.[1]

His concluding words introduce us to something equally important.

The power of example

All leadership is ultimately about being able to say, 'Follow me'. As someone said, 'Example is not a way to lead – it is the only way to lead'. Questions present themselves to those who accept responsibility for leading a discipling community. Am I personally accountable? Is that accountability authentic? Is my heart open to input into my own life?

Do I have a teachable spirit? Am I willing to admit mistakes? Can I ask the people I lead for forgiveness when I get it wrong?

Servant leaders will always have people around them. They will value the safety and security to be found in open relationship with other leaders, and the church will be aware of this. But there will be a characteristic openness with the church too, rather than sharing only and always from a position of strength. It is not easy to connect with a leader who appears to live their entire Christian life at an altitude of 10,000 feet, or thereabouts. Servant hearted leaders will not only share successes and achievements, but will, when appropriate, be willing to disclose times of weakness or moments of stumbling, so that they can also witness to their own experience of mercy, uplifting grace and new victories.

Others are able to identify with us and follow our lead when they see in us, as leaders, openness and vulnerability, alongside a walk with the Lord in which, by his grace, we have been learning to receive his strength in our weakness and to live more consistently in the Spirit. Jesus said, 'I know my sheep and *my sheep know me* – just as the Father knows me and I know the Father' (John 10:14–15, italics mine).

Wise leaders accept the responsibility of earning trust. Trust is a delicate thing and is such a key element in the relationship between a church and its leaders. Trust is not something we can demand. Trust doesn't come about because the structure calls for it. We earn trust as others come to see in us integrity and transparency. First we trust the person, then, as we recognise an anointing on their ministry, we come to trust their ministry also. When the spirit and practice of discipleship characterise the leadership team, the way is open to lead the church community along a similar path. Then, like Jesus, leaders can wash the feet of others by helping them, also, to follow Christ.

Only servant leadership can be trusted to lead the way in forming and facilitating a discipling community.

A culture of servant leadership – *reflections*

For leaders

- Do you agree, or disagree, with the statement, 'The kingdom of God is not a democracy and neither is the church … the issue is the nature of power'? If you see it differently, how would you summarise your understanding?

- What do you make of Menno Simons' observations about spiritual authority, as distinct from the structural authority of a formal role?

- In the light of Jesus' example of servant leadership, how do you think your church perceives the way you lead? (If you don't really know you might want to ask them.)

- In view of our calling to 'go and make disciples', how would others regard your own example in areas like:
    - Personal accountability
    - A teachable spirit
    - Openness with the church
    - Asking forgiveness
    - Earning trust

[1] Tom Marshall, *Understanding Leadership* (Sovereign World, 1991) p111.

Chapter Fifteen
A culture of empowerment and release

A passion to empower

In Jesus' Masterclass we saw that his model of discipling others was personal, relational, affirming, longer term and excitingly productive. To see such strategic discipleship established we need leaders who not only lead the way by example, but who are also passionate about empowering and releasing every single member of the body; leaders who recognise that everyone has deep, sometimes long-held aspirations and dreams; leaders who see destiny written on every face – a destiny birthed in God's love and shaped by the genius of the Holy Spirit – and who lay down their own lives to see those destinies fulfilled. In short, leaders who understand that we will not get the job done until the whole body of Christ is mobilised the way Jesus intended. Discipleship is about empowering and releasing others.

People-centred leadership

People-centred leaders look into people's eyes and see their potential for greatness; and they will serve God and his people to see those faces shine with the joy of fulfilment and fruitfulness. People-centred leaders put people before their own ministry and personal goals. People-centred leaders hold their leadership in trust for a God who loves with a passion the people they lead. Describing David – shepherd boy turned king and national leader, entrusted with God's inheritance, Asaph said:

140

'He cared for them with a true heart and led them with skillful hands' (Psa. 78:72, NLT). First the true heart, *then* the leadership skills.

We are not likely to be good leaders if we haven't settled the issue of our own identity and value. Leadership is not for those who are looking to prove something, to themselves or others. It's not about finding self-worth, or ministry opportunities, much less empires. It's about *people*, and achieving together our God-given mission.

When we establish a network of discipleship across the church community we open up new horizons for every member of the body. Potential can be translated into fulfilment, dreams into reality, blossoming disciples into the new leaders we need, whether in society or in the church. Nothing will give us more delight than to see those in whom we are investing overtake us and forge ahead, blazing new trails for the kingdom. For people-centred leaders, empowering and releasing others is food and drink; it stimulates and satisfies. They know that it carries the kingdom forward because it is every Christian, scattered across the wider community, in their neighbourhood or place of work, who is actually on the front line in society, where light meets darkness and love meets pain.

And it pleases God, who places a call upon the life of each of his children.

A strategy to empower

1. A confident foundation

We begin with the confidence of knowing that a cascade of gifts and talents has been showered liberally on the whole body of Christ by the Holy Spirit. Peterson's rendering of 1 Corinthians 12:4–7 leads to an exuberant conclusion, which captures the generosity of God's giving:

> God's various gifts are handed out everywhere; but they all
> originate in God's Spirit. God's various ministries are carried
> out everywhere; but they all originate in God's Spirit. God's
> various expressions of power are in action everywhere;

but God himself is behind it all. Each person is given
something to do that shows who God is: Everyone gets in on
it, everyone benefits. All kinds of things are handed out by the
Spirit, and to all kinds of people! The variety is wonderful

(1 Cor. 12:4–7, *The Message*)

What a resource! What potential to release! And what a responsibility for leaders to see that everyone has the opportunity to be equipped and enabled! If I as a leader am not focused on the empowerment and release of every member of the body, I am not only short-sighted but likely to be in serious trouble with the Holy Spirit. Strategic discipleship is the God-given pathway to a fully functioning body. We can have confidence that a desire to empower is close to the heart of God. A reluctance to do so would grieve the Spirit who gives those gifts for a purpose.

2. An intentional development process

To the servant heart and the true shepherd, empowering the people for whom they care comes naturally; discipleship will radiate outwards, through team leaders and teams, embracing the whole church. They will believe in people, invest in them and spend time with them. They will make sure that unspoken aspirations are teased out and latent gifts are identified. They will encourage, train and support. They will make space for them to function and delegate authority in appropriate ways. They will take risks, but watch over the development process, praising their successes and helping them to work through their failures. They will not be satisfied until disciples have become fully functioning members of the body, worshipping, growing, witnessing and having an influence in society.

3. An inspiration for the small group dynamic

Many churches are committed to the importance of small groups, whether for fellowship and prayer, for care of the individual, or as an opportunity to follow up what is happening in the corporate life of the church. The danger is that, in practice, groups can sometimes become introspective and drift into a lack of vision or purpose. When that happens, mediocrity beckons. But where there is an overall strategy of intentional discipleship and mission-based objectives, small groups represent a great opportunity.

The group can become a hub of discipleship. If the group's leader, or joint leaders, are themselves accountable, are being discipled and trained for the task, then the group has brilliant opportunities for effective discipling. And if the group leadership includes both pastoral and mission-oriented gifting, then the potential becomes truly exciting. Mission shaped small groups have the opportunity to create initiatives in the surrounding community which are unique to its makeup, relationships and points of access.

4. A corporate vision harmonised with personal discipleship

Visionary church leaders are never happier than when they are initiating something, forging a new path or breaking through into new spaces. But if they have understood the Master's call, they, too, will also recognise the importance of discipling and developing people. That is why breakthrough leaders need to work in a team with others – ministries that can equip the people who will be needed to establish the ground as they go, and build the resources that will support further advance. If a leader becomes vision-driven to the exclusion of all else, the danger is that people in the church may begin to feel like vision fodder and lose a sense of value or purpose. Discipleship has the opposite effect. Corporate vision and the personal growth of each member of the body complement each other – they are equally crucial to success.

The first challenge of the leader with a vision is to gain ownership of that vision across the whole body. That is a process of prayerful dialogue, encouraging others to hear God for themselves; listening well to feedback, taking account of other contributions and ultimately giving a lead, so that the church can move forward together.

The second challenge is to find ways of facilitating everyone's personal growth and development, and then harmonising their input with the corporate vision. I remember a poll which once concluded that, 'Only 20% of 1.7 million employees from 63 countries believe that they have an opportunity to do what they do best every day'. I found that surprising but quite sad. Leadership which empowers has as its aim the harnessing of each individual's personal bent to the overall mission in a can-do atmosphere.

There will always be healthy diversity within the body of Christ, differing concerns and gifts. We welcome that diversity because we need one another's unique contribution. And when there is the security of ongoing committed and accountable relationships, it is a joy to empower and release those who are ready to forge ahead in their particular part of God's plan.

Empowered and released – for the kingdom mission

Jesus' discipleship of the Twelve was outward looking from the start. He talked about the God-centred life, about worship, about character and attitudes. But the entire process of discipleship was in the context of active, ongoing mission. Jesus and the Twelve were mostly on the move, either surrounded *by* people or going *to* people. Times of private training were fitted between Jesus' constant engagement with the needy and the spiritually hungry. The rest of their training was on the job. In the face of human suffering, Jesus was constantly being moved by compassion; in the face of prejudice, he was forever breaking new ground, pushing through society's barriers, reaching people in situations which were isolated hitherto. The mission was paramount for the One who had come to save the lost ones. The interaction between training his disciples and proclaiming the kingdom of God was continuous.

Not surprisingly, Peter caught the same passion. It was first spoken into his life (and his brother, Andrew's) by Jesus' prophetic call: 'Come, follow me ... and I will send you out to fish for people' (Mark 1:17–18). His fervour was displayed on the day of Pentecost and in the challenging events that followed. Whether Peter was engaged in healing the sick on the city streets, or preaching the good news high and low in Jerusalem, he was totally committed to the kingdom mission.

Reading the early chapters of Acts, we are impacted by Peter's leading role as an ambassador of the kingdom and his fearlessness in proclaiming the message. Sometimes on the streets, sometimes before the high priest and the whole council; once being flogged, once imprisoned facing certain death. Over and over again, we find him declaring that the Jesus whom they had crucified had been raised from the dead and given glory by the God of their ancestors; and that only in the name of Jesus Christ of Nazareth could salvation be found. In those years with Jesus, Peter had lived in an atmosphere of radical love and compassion, an environment of all-out mission; he had listened, watched and served day after day until the mission spirit of the Master captured and possessed him, also.

Luke's final mention of Peter's public activities (apart from his contribution to the Council at Jerusalem) is the account of his deliverance from Herod's prison in Acts 12. The last verse of the chapter positions Saul and Barnabas at Antioch, ready for their apostolic calling and sending out by the Holy Spirit in Chapter 13. From then on Paul will be the main character in the book. But the penultimate verses of Chapter 12 (vv23–24) give us something like a status report at that major transitional point in the mission of the Early Church:

> *an angel of the Lord struck [Herod] down … But the word of God continued to spread and flourish.*

> **(Acts 12:23–24)**

Opposition was continuing, but the Jerusalem church had grown rapidly. Witness to Jesus had spread far beyond the city until there were churches across Judea, Galilee and Samaria, and as far north as Antioch in Syria. The door had been opened to the Gentiles at Caesarea and their inclusion endorsed by the Jerusalem elders. Peter's primary calling had been fulfilled – the mission was well under way. He will continue to travel and will also write, while the focus passes to others –

James in Jerusalem and Paul among the Gentiles. But Peter had done a good job. He never lost sight of the mission.

As we pursue the potential of empowering and releasing the body of Christ, our vision centres on the advance of the kingdom – a church carrying the values of the King into every corner of society, demonstrating the love of Jesus in the places of need, proclaiming the good news, and inviting all to become disciples of the One who is both Saviour and Lord.

Go and make disciples

And so we come full circle to where we began – the Commission given by Jesus to his disciples.

> *All authority in heaven and on earth has been given to me.*
> *Therefore go and make disciples of all nations, baptising them*
> *in the name of the Father and of the Son and of the Holy Spirit,*
> *and teaching them to obey everything I have commanded you.*
> *And surely I am with you always, to the very end of the age.*
>
> **(Matt. 28:18–20)**

The challenge for our generation rests with us. Because culture is ultimately set by leaders, they have a particular responsibility to lead the way, but for us all, the call of Jesus to radical discipleship rings clear and true. It is also an exciting message for countless young people today who are ready to put everything on the line for the kingdom of God. For others who, over the years – perhaps imperceptibly – may have settled for something less, or woken up one day and wondered what happened to their first love, it is a fresh challenge from the One whose love never changes.

The Master still calls and his grace is still outrageous.

Bonhoeffer concluded: 'Only Jesus Christ, who bids us follow him, knows the journey's end. But we do know that it will be a road of boundless mercy. Discipleship means joy.'[1]

A culture of empowerment and release – *reflections*

For leaders

- What strategy is in place for a development process that is Spirit-breathed and flexible, but also inclusive and intentional?

- What relationships could be pursued, or encouraged, to facilitate fruitful 'joints of supply' in the body of Christ?

- How are you finding ways of bringing together the development of people and your focus on the mission?

- If your church has a small group strategy, would this be an opportunity to review and redefine the groups' identity and purpose? Could group leaders be inspired and helped towards new levels of Spirit-led creativity in discipleship and outreach?

- What do you find are the biggest challenges for leaders in prioritising time? At your next team retreat, why not reflect on the values demonstrated by the life of Jesus, his relationship with his disciples, and the mission he pursued? It might lead you to consider adjusting priorities, so you can more effectively invest in others what God has given you.

- Be encouraged! The Spirit of God is at work everywhere and you are part of the plan!

[1] Dietrich Bonhoeffer, *The Cost of Discipleship* (Translation by SCM Press, 2001) pxxxiv.

smallGroup central

All of our small group ideas and resources in one place.

Small Group Central is packed with clear, easy to use inspiration for your group. You will find:

- **Free teaching:** Andy Peck, a CWR tutor, has created videos on the practicalities of leading a small group
- **Free tools:** templates, discussion starters, icebreakers – all you need to lead a group study effectively
- **Resources:** books, booklets and DVDs on an extensive list of themes, Bible books and life issues.

Log on and find out more at
www.smallgroupcentral.org.uk

cover to **cover**

vital:

Life EVERY DAY

SMALL GROUP **ToolBox**

Every Day with Jesus

Daily encouragement from God's Word.

Our compact, daily Bible reading notes for adults are published bimonthly and offer a focus for every need. They are available as individual issues or annual subscriptions, in print, in eBook format or by email.

Every Day with Jesus

With around half a million readers, this insightful devotional by Selwyn Hughes is one of the most popular daily Bible reading tools in the world. A large-print edition is also available.
72-page booklets, 120x170mm

Inspiring Women Every Day

Written by women for women to inspire, encourage and strengthen.
64-page booklets, 120x170mm

Life Every Day

Apply the Bible to life each day with these challenging life-application notes written by international speaker and well-known author Jeff Lucas.
64-page booklets, 120x170mm

Cover to Cover Every Day

Study one Old Testament and one New Testament book in depth with each issue, and a psalm every weekend. Two well-known Bible scholars each contribute a month's series of daily Bible studies. Covers every book of the Bible in five years.
64-page booklets, 120x170mm

Courses and seminars

Publishing and media

Conference facilities

Transforming lives

CWR's vision is to enable people to experience personal transformation through applying God's Word to their lives and relationships.

Our Bible-based training and resources help people around the world to:
• Grow in their walk with God
• Understand and apply Scripture to their lives
• Resource themselves and their church
• Develop pastoral care and counselling skills
• Train for leadership
• Strengthen relationships, marriage and family life and much more.

Our insightful writers provide daily Bible-reading notes and other resources for all ages, and our experienced course designers and presenters have gained an international reputation for excellence and effectiveness.

CWR's Training and Conference Centres in Surrey and East Sussex, England, provide excellent facilities in idyllic settings - ideal for both learning and spiritual refreshment.

CWR Applying God's Word
to everyday life and relationships

WR, Waverley Abbey House,
averley Lane, Farnham,
urrey GU9 8EP, UK

elephone: **+44 (0)1252 784700**
mail: **info@cwr.org.uk**
ebsite: **www.cwr.org.uk**

egistered Charity No 294387
ompany Registration No 1990308